ROBBING PETER TO PAY PAUL

JV Huffman Jr.

ISBN 979-8-89043-140-0 (paperback)
ISBN 979-8-89043-141-7 (digital)

Christian Faith Publishing
832 Park Avenue
Meadville, PA 16335
www.christianfaithpublishing.com

Printed in the United States of America

To God, Gilda, Joshua, Emily, Hannah,
Judge, and the over five hundred victims.

Introduction

I am writing this book for some very specific reasons. Please keep these in mind as you read and filter everything through these principles:

1. *Honor God.* Athanasius, a fourth-century teacher born in Egypt, trained in Greece, said, "The only system of thought into which Jesus Christ will fit is the one in which He is the starting point."

   Every aspect of our lives should be governed by this principle. The Holy Bible, God's inerrant and infallible Word, as expressed through the life, death, and resurrection of Jesus Christ, proclaims the greatest commandment of God is to "love the Lord your God with all your heart and with all your soul and with all your mind" (Matthew 22:37 ESV).

   What else is honor but to live this way?

   If I had been living a God-honoring life in every area of my life, I would not be where I am today, and hundreds of people across the US would not have lost millions of dollars.

   Alas, not all is lost. With God, there is a new beginning, a chance to begin honoring him from this point forward. It is here he begins to bless anew.

2. *Accept responsibility.* One of the many great life lessons my parents taught me that my wife and I have taught our children is to accept responsibility for your actions. As far back as I can remember, my parents always held me accountable

to this principle. I have done this throughout the whole process of events since November 2008. This book is part of that ongoing process.

3. *Set the record straight (accuracy).* I never knew such dishonest media and justice systems existed in our country. There were so many lies, assumptions, and rumors flying around following my arrest that it was a fulltime job trying to keep score, and it still is. Every time I read something in the papers, there are inaccuracies and opinions quoted as facts. I will try to unravel the mystery and misconceptions. I also know how much this principle is an oxymoron coming from someone who lived such an erroneous life for seventeen years.

4. *Understand.* This one is the hardest for people who know me—the why. I think this one principle will bring the most healing, and yet some of it defies any logic. It is even hard for me to understand the why.

5. *Educate.* This one goes hand in hand with "Understand," but it also goes further. I hope by educating people, they will be better equipped to see traps and avoid them, either in becoming enslaved to sin or from being deceived and suffering as so many have already.

There may be times as you read when it seems like I am whining, seeking pity or sympathy, or rationalizing my actions, but I am not. I mention it here to stave off these assumptions. I am trying to be accurate and honest in every way. Some things I have to say are hard—hard for me to say and hard for some people to hear. However, they need to be said. I make no apologies for them.

I have set these points as my standard to judge each piece of this work. If something did not meet the standard, I either deleted it or reworked it so it would. The first standard, "Honor God," was the only principle the entire work had to meet. If something accurately met one of the other standards but was not honoring God, I reworked it.

It is my sincere desire and prayer that God will use this book to change many lives and draw them unto Him.

I also hope and pray this book will bring peace, forgiveness, freedom, understanding, and closure to the hundreds of people who lost money and have suffered emotionally, physically, and spiritually because of my iniquity.

I am truly sorry and seek your forgiveness, and I desire to be reconciled to each of you in Jesus Christ.

Charles was born in 1882 and died in 1949. In 1920, he started a company to scam customers by paying early investors a return using later investor's money. The company collapsed after just one year. He was not the first to try such a scheme; however, his attempt was so prominent during his time that the scheme would forever become known by his name. All similar schemes are labeled *Ponzi* schemes after Charles Ponzi.

The confession of evil works is the first beginning of good works.

—Augustine

A man who confesses his sins in the presence of a brother
knows that he is no longer alone with himself; he experiences
the presence of God in the reality of the other person.

—Dietrich Bonhoeffer

Confession is a radical reliance on grace. A proclamation of our
trust in God's goodness… If our understanding of grace is small,
our confession will be small… The power of confession lies
not with the person who makes it but the God who hears it.

—Max Lucado

In November 1991, I had a dream for the creation of a new investment company to help people achieve their financial goals in life. I founded the Biltmore Financial Group that month with one client and a lot of ambition. The business grew slowly but not enough to be viable on its own. My personal financial position was already precarious when I started the business and only got worse as I struggled to keep it going. My pride and unwillingness to admit failure to anyone led me down a path of total destruction. I was the company. I had an exceptional reputation in the community and was from a family with a long history of integrity. There were no other employees, and there were no real checks and balances in place to hold me accountable.

One of the first things you learn in accounting class is the need to have checks and balances. Every part of our lives needs checks and balances to hold us accountable. God requires His children to have a higher standard than that of the world, and without having proper checks and balances, the tendency is to go astray.

That is the long and short of what happened to me. I began way back in November of 1991 with all good intentions, never even thinking about doing anything illegal. However, financial difficulties coupled with pride and no accountability will cloud one's judgment. I cannot begin to pinpoint an exact time when that happened. I just know, looking back, that it did.

This is the part in most stories where we shift the blame to Satan and say, "The devil made me do it," but I cannot even say that. He often tempts us, confuses our thinking, and helps us rationalize the sins in our lives; but initially, in this early stage, he did not have to do anything except stand back and watch as I did it to myself.

I have always been a very independent, private person. My wife would tell you I keep everything very close to my chest. I hate asking for directions. I would rather wander around lost for hours before admitting I am lost and ask for help. This was no different. Satan was certainly standing by ready to help me with my sin, if need be. Later on, as that sin grew, he did just that; but initially it was all me, all my fault. For seventeen years, I lived with this monkey—no, this *gorilla*—on my back. Monkeys are small and not all that hard to carry. Yet this felt more like an enormous silverback male gorilla; truly, I was carrying King Kong.

I am serving a 30–40 1/2–year prison sentence in the North Carolina Department of Public Safety's Division of Prisons (DOP) for securities fraud and obtaining property by false pretense. I will be seventy-five years old at the earliest possible release date, November 2038.

*****

Friday, November 7, 2008, you could say my world both ended and began anew. That was the day the North Carolina secretary of state's agents showed up in force at my home office with a search warrant. I left my house that night in handcuffs, never to return, having signed everything we owned over to the Securities and Exchange Commission (SEC). My wife and four children were to receive a one-time sum of $15,000, their clothes, and personal items. They were homeless and without a provider.

It was a normal day. We homeschooled all our children, Gilda, Hannah, and Judge. Emily was at college, and Joshua was traveling from college to Charleston, South Carolina, to spend the weekend with friends. I was in my office with two clients, signing paperwork to transfer ownership of a condo to my company, the Biltmore Financial Group (BFG), in exchange for money added to their account. As we were about to finish up, there came a knock at the door.

I was not expecting other clients, so I was at a loss as to who it could be. Gilda, the kids, or the men working for me around the house would never interrupt me while I was with a client unless it was an emergency. Even then, Gilda would page me on the phone from inside the house.

I opened the door to find a gentleman wearing a jacket with "NC Secretary of State" printed on the back, a gun on his side, and my guess of maybe eight people standing in my front driveway. He introduced himself as Agent Sean Pruett and presented me with a search warrant as I stepped outside and closed the door, leaving my clients alone in the office.

This was a new experience for me, never having been in any kind of trouble with the law in the past. The only other time I had been served with legal papers was during my six-year tenure on the Catawba County Board of Education when someone sued the board and each board member individually. However, this time was not a surprise.

This was the event I had anticipated, dreaded, and ironically looked forward to for many years. I had anticipated it, knowing it was inevitable. I had dreaded it, knowing the consequences it would bring. I had looked forward to it, knowing it would be the end of the tragic slavery to sin that had so consumed my life.

Agent Pruett allowed me to close the meeting with the clients, and then we resumed our business together. Although he and I had never met before that day, we knew who each other was. He had been investigating BFG since sometime before February 2008. At least that is when I became aware of it. I also knew he had driven by my house at least once during the past eight months.

I wondered all the time, as I am certain everyone in that situation would, how the downfall would take place, and what chain of events would be the impetus to cause it all to unravel.

*****

I am not sure of the exact date, but sometime prior to February 2008, things were innocently enough set into motion. Two of my clients—business owners, husband and wife—unbeknownst to them, launched the snowball over the edge that would cause the avalanche of my life.

It was time for their periodic review with their financial planner. Included in all the accounting data were information and statements on their accounts with BFG. As the financial planner studied the data, he became suspicious of the great returns my clients were receiving on their statements. He had never heard of BFG, so he sent off the information to the North Carolina secretary of state, without my clients' permission. At that point, there was no stopping it.

When he told my clients what he had done, they were not pleased. We were friends and fellow church members. We loved each other. Their daughter was part of the college ministry I was involved with at our church. I was there for them as they struggled through some difficult times.

They felt they had betrayed our friendship. When the husband was finally able to talk with me and explain what had happened, more than he could ever know at that point, I understood fully his feelings of having betrayed a friend.

They were like so many of my clients—friends, friends' family members, relatives of mine, and fellow church members. We were not friends when they first approached me about opening an account with BFG, but I did know their daughter very well. Many times in my life, the old saying "God works in mysterious ways" has proven true. I know they may only see our relationship now based on the business we did together and think of it as a travesty; however, I have a much broader view, and I hope they may someday as well. I see God bringing us together at a very difficult time in their lives to fill a need for prayer and support and to introduce others to help them as well. Although the losses are tragic, and I feel terrible having trampled on our friendship, I am thankful to have been there for them in matters of much greater importance in life.

Early February 2008, I was in Orlando, Florida, at Universal Studios Resort with my wife and our two youngest children, our best friends and their three children, their sister-in-law from Tennessee and her two children, and two of our best friends from Myrtle Beach, South Carolina.

The first morning at the Universal parks, we had gotten everyone's tickets when my phone rang. I always kept my office phone forwarded to my BlackBerry phone to be able to take care of anything my clients needed while I was out of town. My clients knew I loved to travel and did so often. They also knew they could always get in touch with me if they needed anything to do with their accounts. I always made sure they could have access to them in less than a week if not the same day. They liked that and had peace of mind about the security of their money, knowing they could access it quickly.

This call was from William (not his real name). He had become one of my dearest brothers in Christ. His personal account was sizable, and he had brought several very large accounts to me over the years. He and his wife are strong servants of the Lord. I always enjoyed visiting with them in their home, but I always left with tears in my eyes, sick to my stomach, and depressed. How could I do this to them? How could I lie, cheat, and steal from them, all the while with a smile on my face and a "God bless you" on my lips?

I was standing at the entrance to Universal Studios. I walked away from my crowd of family and friends in order to hear, but also more for privacy. My first thought was that he needed some money from his account. He began by asking if BFG had ever been or was currently under investigation by the North Carolina secretary of state. I immediately felt a tightening in my chest at his question. One of my best abilities, my entire life, has been to think quickly on my feet. I have always been able to analyze situations quickly and respond. Over the prior sixteen years, I had become adept at spinning—selling—any scenario to allay anyone's fears. In other words, I was an expert liar. My mind quickly filled with questions, scenarios, ideas, and possibilities. I was immediately in damage control mode, as well as being overwhelmed with paranoia and feelings of panic attack. However, I could not afford to lose control.

Luckily, in this instance, I did not have to lie again to William. I answered his question truthfully with a no. I honestly did not know of any such investigation, and I told him this was the first I had heard of it if it were true. I asked him how he had come about this information. Understandably, he did not want to divulge the source, because it was told to him in confidence, and he did not have permission to share that with anyone.

William's call had two purposes: first, to check on the validity of the rumor, along with the security of his money; and most likely, to give a brother in Christ a heads up. William, like all my clients, trusted me fully. He and I were kindred spirits in our Lord Jesus Christ. As part of the Church, the body of Christ, we are supposed to look out for one another. We are called to hold one another accountable, to support one another, to protect one another's interests. William was living out his faith and was being a true example of how a Christian should handle a situation, and I was failing miserably at doing the same.

The next thing he said cut me to my soul. He said that because we were Christian brothers, he trusted me to be truthful with him, and if I told him everything was okay, then he was satisfied. My chest became even tighter, my breathing shorter. The enormity of the fear was overwhelming. It was good I was sitting down, or I may have fallen over. I wanted to yell out to him the horrible truth. I wanted to confess to him. I truly loved this man, and I even knew in my heart he would not condemn me but love me unconditionally with the love of Christ. He was one of only a handful of people I truly felt I could confess to and receive back unconditional love and forgiveness and understanding, but I did not confess. I could not. There was too much at stake, too many people would be hurt.

If I told even one person, it would all fall apart. I could not tell someone and ask him or her to keep it a secret. That would have made them an accomplice. No way could I risk incriminating anyone else. I did what I always did and remained calm in appearance. I kept my voice positive and confident. I lied through my teeth once again. I felt like the whole world was closing in on me, as if everyone around me suddenly knew the truth and was looking at me, pointing fingers, and whispering about me. I expected a SWAT team to surround me, throw me on the ground, and haul me off in handcuffs.

I think the apostle Peter could empathize with my feelings of paranoia and panic at this point. All four Gospels—Matthew, Mark, Luke, and John—give accounts of Peter's denial of Christ. John adds in his Gospel, after Jesus's arrest, he (John) talked to the servant girl watching over the door, allowing or denying access to the courtyard of the high priest, so she would grant Peter entrance. John says he knew the high priest, implying a relationship, a familiarity. That being the case, the servant girl would have recognized John. She would have surely known him to be a disciple of Jesus. What else would John have told her to gain access for Peter except that he was with him? Peter was not a stupid man—a bit impetuous, hot-tempered, tending to engage his mouth before engaging his brain, but not stupid. He had to know what John told the girl to vouch for him at the gate. He must have been fearful and apprehensive, paranoid of arrest.

Whether we are willing to admit it or not, we can all identify with Peter on some level. We all tend to talk big about how we would act given various situations. "No, Lord! Not me! Those others may abandon You, but never me! I will fight to the death for You!" Is not that what Peter said in so many words to Jesus? But when the chips were down, what did he do? When he felt the fear, panic, paranoia, pressure on his chest, and shortness of breath…when he saw the eyes looking at him all around, the fingers pointing…and when he heard the whispers being spoken, all these began taking their toll on him. What did Peter do? He caved to the pressure, and he denied Christ.

It is easy for us to say, "If I were Peter, I would never have done that." Be careful what you say. Be careful not to be judgmental of how Peter acted. I think Jesus said it best, "Let him who is without sin cast the first stone." Admit it or not, we have all experienced what Peter felt, and more likely than not, we often cave to the pressure as well.

Luke's account is the only one that says when Peter denied Christ for the third time and the rooster crowed, Jesus turned and looked at Peter. Then Peter left and wept bitterly. Those were the eyes of God looking at Peter. What kind of eyes would they have been? Angry eyes? Condemning eyes? Disgusted eyes?

No, Peter was one of God's children, set apart in Christ before the beginning of everything. God looked at Peter, His child, with loving, compassionate, merciful, understanding, and forgiving eyes. I believe Peter knew, with all his heart, the message Jesus conveyed to him in that look. And I believe, because Peter knew how fully and unconditionally Jesus loved him and forgave him, he hated himself and what he had done all the more. He knew there was nothing about himself that would ever make him worthy of such love.

That is how I felt there in Florida, talking to William on the phone. I hated myself and what I was doing to William and all the other clients, to my family, friends, church, community, and the list could go on. However, the one I hated doing it to the most was Christ.

I am sure when Peter was weeping bitterly after his denial of Christ, he was asking himself, "What have I done? How could I so easily and quickly deny Jesus, not just once but three times? And that look of love! How could Jesus love me after what I did?"

I understand Peter, and he understands me, but more importantly, Jesus understands us both, and He understands whatever your denial is, as well. He looks at us all through the same eyes He looks at Peter. They convey the same message to us: "I forgive you, and I love you."

At that point, I literally wanted to die, but that would have been the coward's way out. That would have ended the suffering in this world, but it would have left my family to deal with the aftermath of the horrible truth. Oh, it would have solved some things quite well. I carried a $20 million life insurance policy on myself that would have more than taken care of paying everything back, but I could not do that to those left to clean up the mess. I also knew, deep in my heart, that was not what God wanted, either. I knew He was not finished with me yet. I still had things to do for Him.

Knowing that truth did not keep me from hating myself for what I had done, for what I had become, for what I had allowed sin to become in my life, for selling out to sin. God talks to us in His Word about the spiritual battle we are in and about the battle between the flesh and the spirit within us. Up to this point, I had never felt these battles raging in my life as intensely as I did there at the entrance to Universal Studios.

In the sixteen years since the beginning of BFG, I experienced the same feelings of regret, remorse, sorrow, depression, conviction, etcetera, etcetera. You name it, and I was feeling it. I would continue feeling it daily, right up until November 7, 2008. Like a tide, they would ebb and flow, but always they were there, increasing in intensity over time. As the pit grew deeper, darker, more complicated, and hopeless, so did all the different feelings.

William was appeased, and with the call now completed, I began the task of gathering myself. Time to put on the happy, "All is perfect in the world" face, and return to the crowd waiting for me to begin our day of fun and adventure in the parks. All the while, every waking minute, and even in my sleep, what little there was, my mind churned with all the possibilities of what was happening. I kept trying to put together a trail of recent events or people that might have led to the North Carolina secretary of state investigating BFG.

I knew of at least two people, one a bookkeeper who had worked for my family's business for over thirty years, and the other an insurance/investment salesperson, whom I had known for over twenty years. Neither of which did I think William knew. The bookkeeper also completed the tax returns for other BFG clients. He and I had never seen eye to eye on many levels. He had a very explosive temper, and we had, on occasion, voiced our dislike of one another. Now we both had something in common—being convicted felons. I will give him credit for trying to warn people they were eventually going to lose their money. The other man was just angry and greedy because many of his clients had moved money from his business to BFG. Eventually, his shady business dealings caught up with him as well, and he lost his job.

Both men would have been at the top of my suspect list, but I could not confirm either right away, nor could I figure out their connection to William. The bookkeeper's involvement became known months later during the summer of 2008. Neither of these men was the impetus of the investigation, but both eagerly got involved. After I had already pieced together the chain of events that got the investigation started, that summer, a close friend came to my office one afternoon to warn me the bookkeeper was trying desperately to convince one of my relatives to talk to the investigating agent, Sean Pruitt, to help him gain information secretly.

At that point, not too many people knew of the investigation. I am not sure if this relative told anyone else they were being recruited. They claimed to be really struggling with what to do and eventually declined to get involved. I could not have held it against them had they decided the other way. The outcome would have been the same. I sincerely apologize for having put this person in that situation, because it is clearly my fault, and I ask them for forgiveness.

The rest of our time in Florida was uneventful and very stressful for me. Everyone else had a wonderful time. I remember how much I did not want to return home. I did not know what was awaiting me. I was fairly sure there would not be a long line of clients waiting at my office door to get their money. If any of them were panicking, they would have called me and asked for their money. However, I did not know if I would return home to the SWAT team waiting at my house.

We arrived home in Catawba County to nothing out of the ordinary, but the stress remained. Every time the phone rang, I could feel my blood pressure rise, and I would become nauseous. I wanted to avoid all contact with the world. The paranoia and depression grew daily. I withdrew more and more from everything over the next nine months. I would hide out in my office alone, claiming to be working; but in reality, I was sitting in a daze, numb to everything around me. I was fearful of the phone, cars passing by on the road, email alerts, and other things. Many days I would claim to have clients to see and just go driving around. Sometimes I would go to the YMCA or the spa at Rock Barn Club and sit in the steam room or sauna. I felt these were places where no one could find me. I contemplated suicide often.

By the time we returned home, I still had not figured out how William had come about his information, but it would not be long before I did. When my friends from church finally caught up with me and told me what had happened with their financial planner, everything began to make sense. They were distraught, thinking they had betrayed our friendship and caused me undue scrutiny from a government agency. They were very apologetic. I assured them there was no reason to worry.

Now I had a better understanding of what happened and how William found out. Once I started thinking about it, I remembered how both William and the friends from church became clients. The same person referred them both to BFG. This person was William's close friend and worked for my two friends in their business.

Now it all made some sense, but it did nothing to ease the pressure. On the contrary, it only added to it. Knowing how they were connected started me thinking about how many other clients they knew. This was only adding more to the stress. By this time, BFG had over five hundred clients all over the United States, and it was mind-boggling how interconnected they were.

Over the years, I never did any advertising just for the sake of drumming up new business. What little advertising I did do was for things that showed support for the local community—ball teams, scouting events, schools, or charities. It was always to help them, never for the advertising.

All my clients were so happy with their return on investment they were constantly sending me new clients. Through the years, there were times when money would be running extremely low, and I would offer special bonuses to existing clients if they referred someone new. As I did this more, the current clients expected the bonuses. I hated having to do anything to encourage new clients because I hated everything to do with BFG, but I was trapped. I had to keep it going. As long as it appeared successful and everyone was happy, I convinced myself there was hope of coming up with a way to get out without anyone knowing the truth or getting hurt. However, deep down I knew that would never happen. I knew that was not how God operated. He would hold me accountable, and so I turned a blind eye and a deaf ear to the truth. Like Jonah in the Bible, I ran in the opposite direction, one leading deeper into bondage. The thing about a Ponzi scheme is it is a living, growing monster. You have to feed it new investors all the time for it to survive.

As businesses go, the last twelve months of BFG were very successful, if you look at revenue. I believe, by the end of the first quarter of 2008, there was approximately $3 million in the bank. By November 2008, I think there was less than $400,000. In the early months of 2008, I was comfortable that I could contain this with William and my friends. I could put off the inevitable, and it appeared I had; not that the pressure eased up any, but I still clung to the hope of finding a solution. What a fool I was!

The seeming success of cash flow was not a result of my drumming up business. What most people did not understand was how eager people were to give me money. Over the years, word-of-mouth advertising had brought in clients from all over the country. People would call up and say they knew one of my clients and that person had done business with me for years. They would say their friend had no clue how I made money but was thrilled with their returns and felt safe and trusted me implicitly. That was good enough for the new person. They would say they did not care to understand either, as long as they got the same returns and security. The next thing they would say is they had $100,000 or $250,000 or $500,000 or whatever amount they wanted to send me.

This stuff is so crazy and twisted when you think about it. This is how it worked. I had over five hundred clients, nearly all connected in some way, by family relations, friendships, or acquaintances. If just a handful became disillusioned, the whole thing would unravel. That was a huge part of the trap Satan had me in. There was no possible way to ease out of the business, and no possible way to turn down a new client.

If I were to tell a potential client I could not invest their money, what do you think would be the first thing they would do? They would call up their friend, my current client, and tell them I would not take their money. Now what is the first thing my current client is going to think? They are going to ask themselves, "Why will he not take on a new client?" Then they would probably begin to doubt the security of their money. After all, what successful business does not want to grow? Next, they are going to call their friends who are investors of BFG and ask them what they think. Then I start getting calls. Then they start thinking, maybe it is time to move their money somewhere else, and they lose confidence in BFG. The next thing I know, there is a rush by all my clients to move their money, which no longer exists.

If everything were liquidated at fair market value, there would be a considerable sum of money, but only a fraction of the investors' total account values. It would be similar to a run on a bank. I am assuming we all know banks only keep enough cash on hand to operate day to day. That is a mere fraction of total deposits. If all of a bank's depositors showed up demanding their money, no bank could honor all their requests.

Proverbs 22:1 says, "A good name is to be chosen rather than great riches, and favor is better than silver or gold." All my clients' confidence was false confidence. My good name and reputation; a good name and reputation I had destroyed misled them. No one knew I had destroyed it, and that too was part of the trap. I was so scared of what the truth would do to hurt my family's name and reputation that I was willing to do whatever it took to keep the truth hidden.

I am not trying to pass the blame on to the clients. They have to be responsible for their part, and I have to stand up and take responsibility for my part, which was deceiving and defrauding every one of the clients. I fully accept that responsibility.

That is a foreign concept to the society we live in today. We all want to shift the blame or responsibility onto someone else. It is not a new concept. What was the first thing Adam said when God questioned him about his sin? He pointed his finger at Eve and blamed her, and we have been doing the same thing ever since.

Life moved on from February 2008 to November 2008. As the year progressed, so did my anxiety. Eventually, as Sean Pruett's investigation progressed, rumors began to surface. I did a *good* job of allaying concerns, as I always had an answer for everything. If someone called, seeming nervous and began talking about removing their money, I acted like it was no big deal and even encouraged them to do so, especially if they were unsure. Most clients had been with me through the unstable financial times following the 9/11 attacks on the US or they knew someone who had, and they remembered the great returns they made while everyone else was losing money. With that in mind, they would calm down and take a wait-and-see attitude, relying on their trust in me. Some did take their money out, but surprisingly few. I rejoiced for those who took the money and ran.

Sean Pruett presented me with a search warrant and explained to me I was not under arrest and was free to leave if I chose. The warrant was to take files, computers, and cell phones. I was numb, terrified, and still in damage control mode. First thing, I had to take care of my family. Gilda, Hannah, and Judge were in the house doing school. The guys who worked for me around the house were working on the addition to my garage. Mr. Pruett asked me if I had a firearm on me or on the premises. I remember thinking, *What an odd thing to ask me.* I did not own any guns. But I quickly began to realize how serious this was. He was concerned for the safety of his officers, for my family, and for me. There were many people on his team, and they all carried guns.

He had already been to the house and talked to my wife before coming to see me in my office. After he talked about firearms, he suggested, for the safety of my family and to make this process as easy as possible, it would be best if my family would go somewhere for the day, and if my workers would leave, as well. I went in the house and talked to Gilda first.

I do not remember exactly when, but sometime between February and November, I told her some of what was going on with the investigation. I painted a favorable picture of this all being a misunderstanding by the friends' financial planner and a conspiracy by the bookkeeper and the other insurance/investment salesperson. She fully believed and trusted me. I told her to take the kids and their schoolwork and go to my parents' house until I called her to return. She hugged me, kissed me, and said she believed in me, and she knew all would be well. She was a woman of incredible faith; she had no clue anything was wrong. With her and the kids taken care of, I went out to send the workers home. I am sure they were clueless about what was happening and had many questions.

At that time, I had five guys who worked for me; three of whom were church members. One was a young man with many personal problems in his life. We were all trying to help him sort through them. The last was my retired uncle who had worked for me for over ten years.

Sean Pruett's boss had accompanied his team that day. I was not sure why at this point. Maybe they were playing "good cop, bad cop" with me, but I knew right off I did not like Sean Pruett, or his arrogant attitude. His boss and I seemed to hit it off from the start. Still, he deferred everything to Agent Pruett, because it was his investigation. Before the day was over, I would learn why I felt more comfortable with his boss—he was a Christian, a man who lived his faith. Sean Pruett may have been a Christian as well, but it did not show in his actions. Maybe he was just being all business in front of his superior.

Sean Pruett again told me I was not under arrest and I did not have to stay there. I was free to leave if I wanted. Of course, I did not intend to leave them alone in my house; however, in hindsight, knowing what I know now about the importance of keeping your mouth shut and having legal counsel, I should have left. On the other hand, looking back, I also see there was not a more perfect way for things to have happened. It was so obvious, God's hand upon it all. Finally, all the running, hiding, lying, and everything was ending. Yet somehow, I was not feeling relieved.

They had been there for some time. I am not sure how long, but it seemed like forever. I do not think it was lunchtime yet. People were all over the office, house, and garage. All of it was making me increasingly nervous. My chest hurt and I could hardly breathe. At one point, in passing and in a snide tone of voice, Sean Pruett made a comment asking if I had been having cash flow problems lately. I remember telling him I really did not care for him or him being there and did not want to talk to him. I walked away and out onto the front porch steps. I took out my BlackBerry because I needed a friend to talk to.

Paul was one of my best friends in life at the time. Ace and Todd were the other two, but Paul was my buddy. We are about the same age and hung out together. We talked every day on BlackBerry Messenger. We traveled together with our wives, who were good friends as well.

Ace was a different kind of friend. He was much older and much wiser, a mentor of sorts. He is deceased now. I never got to speak to him again after I was arrested. He and his wife, Joye, were also clients. I know they were both deeply hurt. Ace had a huge, gentle, servant heart. God had definitely given him the gift of service. Wherever Ace would go, he always saw other people's needs and would go out of his way to serve them, whether he knew them or not. His love for people always inspired me and served to convict me of my sins.

Todd was another kind of best friend. He was younger than me. I was more of his confidant than the other way around. He knew he was safe in sharing anything with me, and he often did. He was my pastor. Pastors have few close friends, especially within the church. They sometimes are the loneliest people in a church.

At that moment in my life, there on the steps of my front porch, I needed my best buddy—Paul. I knew exactly where he was too. Paul worked for an international corporation and regularly traveled the globe on business. Some months prior, I had planned to accompany Paul to Singapore for the first two weeks of November. While he worked, I was going exploring and when he was finished, we were going to go scuba diving. At the last minute, God laid it on my heart to stay home, so I canceled the trip.

Paul was halfway around the world so I knew if it was morning here, it was evening there. On the porch steps, I pinged him on BlackBerry Messenger, "Marco." He replied, "Polo." So I knew he was available to talk. "I need you to pray for me. My world is falling apart." He replied, "What's up? What's happening?" Then one of the agents saw me using my phone and took it from me. I never got the chance to reply.

With my phone gone, I really felt alone. I went to very few places without my phone. I am sure you can relate to that feeling. It's like going through withdrawal. Again, looking back, I can clearly see God's hand controlling everything. That phone was one of the crutches I relied on instead of fully trusting in and leaning on God.

He was stripping me of all my excuses, so there was nothing left but Him.

For years, there was a prayer in my heart I could never muster up the courage to pray, to ask God to end this nightmare in whatever way He saw fit to bring Himself the most glory. A simple prayer of a few words, but one I could not bring myself to pray. Oh, I prayed many times for God to end it, but in a way that no one would be hurt and no one would know the truth. I could not surrender to God what I knew would bring so much pain and loss to so many people. I knew in my heart God could and would use this to bring glory to Himself. Instead, I would pray for Him to give me a secret way out so there would be no pain and loss, knowing He was not going to honor that prayer. Yet I would plead with Him. He is God. He can do anything, "Please don't make me and all these people walk through this valley, this dark night of the soul."

You see, I was not at the lowest point; that point where we are finally ready to surrender all. I understand grace and salvation. I surrendered my heart a lifetime ago. I knew who I was and who I was not. Salvation for me was never a doubt or a question, but the lordship of Christ in my life was. There on the steps of my front porch, I finally gave up the struggle to be in control. I prayed that long-dreaded prayer, and I told God I was ready to end it. His way, whatever He wanted… I was ready! I asked for courage to do whatever He wanted of me.

If you are a Christian, you have to come to that same point of surrender. We talk in church about surrendering your life to Christ, placing your trust in the work of salvation Jesus did on the cross. What we are most often dealing with at that time is accepting the salvation he is offering, believing in who Jesus is. The sad thing is the Church, most of the time, drops the ball from there. Christ, through the Great Commission in Matthew 28:19–20, calls us to make disciples. I am not making light of salvation. That is the eternal gift, for which Christ paid so much to give us, and to accept or reject it is the single most important decision we will make in our life.

The second is to submit to the lordship of Christ in our lives. That may come in some big dramatic, public, cataclysmic way, as it did for me; or it may be a very private, humble, and beautiful thing. Maybe the thing you are surrendering control of would not seem big to someone else, but it is the Goliath in your life. It matters not what it is, but know this fact: It is holding you hostage and deceiving you. It is killing you and hindering you from having the freedom God is offering if you will only let it go, let it burn up in the fire of His all-consuming love for you. He has only your best interest at heart.

Here is the truth of John 10:10–11, "The thief comes only to steal and kill and destroy. I [Christ] came that they [you] may have life and have it abundantly. I am the Good Shepherd. The Good Shepherd lays down his life for the sheep." These are God's words to you. Heed them right now. Do not wait. Begin a walk free from the bondage that has been holding you for so long.

Many who are reading this know what I am talking about because you have "been there, done that." Rejoice in what God has done in your life. Now ask Him to open your eyes to those around you who need to hear this truth and who need freedom. Ask Him to use you to reach out and help them. Ask Him to use you to make disciples.

I got up from those steps and went back into the house to find Sean Pruett's boss. I told him I wanted to sit down one on one with him. The most private place in the house at that moment, which had no agents in it, was the library in the basement.

This was one of my favorite rooms in the house. It was quiet and peaceful. When I added to the house, it was the only room without any media except speakers for music. The walls were lined with bookcases and display cases. We chose an *I Love Lucy* theme for the room. *I Love Lucy* is our family's favorite TV show. For years, I had been an avid *I Love Lucy* collector. The room was filled with anything and everything *Lucy* and my books.

We closed the door and sat on opposite sofas facing each other, and I started spilling my guts. This caught him completely off guard. He had to stop me and go get a pad of paper to take notes. When he came back, I could not shut up. I know I was not thinking clearly. It just felt great to let it all go, to get it out. I was vomiting words. I do not think he had ever had this happen. Being a Christian, he understood what was going on, but he also had a job to do. He did a good job, balancing between being a brother in Christ and an agent for the North Carolina secretary of state.

He asked if I would consent to recording our conversation. Thankfully, I said no, not because I wanted to be able to deny any of it in court, but because any kind of recording can be dangerous in the wrong hands of the media and/or the public. If it ever became a part of the public court documents, I did not want it used to hurt or humiliate my family or the investors. He also asked if I wanted an attorney, and if I did, at any time while we were talking, we would have to stop. I said no, I did not want an attorney. Even if I did, I had no idea where I would get one right then.

We talked for hours. We went to the library sometime in the afternoon, and it was evening when we finished. He asked many questions, and I eagerly answered them all. His notepad was full. It felt good to confess. While sitting there, I remember telling him about the weight I had felt for so long and about the pain in my chest, and about the shortness of breath in my lungs, and how in this moment it had all gone away. I felt tremendous peace. Literally, upon confession, all that lifted off me. The First Epistle of John 1:9 says, "If we confess our sins, He is faithful and just to forgive our sins and to cleanse us from all unrighteousness." That cleansing was what I was experiencing at that moment. As scared as I was, I was not about to stop. It felt great. It felt right. The tears would not stop flowing. The hold, the bondage of sin that Satan had on me, was broken.

Was opening up to this agent the best thing to do? Yes and no. From the perspective of God's sovereignty over all things—yes, it was. From a worldly, legal perspective—no, it was not. If I were being worldly-wise, I would have left as soon as I had taken care of my family and my workers and gone hunting for an attorney. I should have never opened my mouth. I was not under arrest. They were going to take everything they wanted, according to the search warrant, and I could not stop that from happening. However, I was not wise about these things. I had no idea where to look for an attorney with experience in these types of cases. Other than this instance, I had never been involved in anything criminal in my life and never had a need for a criminal attorney. I was clueless about how the criminal justice system worked. Knowing then what I know now, I am not sure I would have done the same thing. However, I am glad, for the most part, that I did not know, because I am afraid that if I had left, I would have lost the courage to pray the prayer and step out in faith to confess.

We talked about everything that had transpired over the past seventeen years. I told him how it was never my intention to defraud anyone. I wanted a legal, successful business back in 1991 when I started. I formed BFG with that goal in mind, but it never became that success. Early on, because of personal financial trouble and mostly pride, I made the fatal decision to use one client's money to "solve" my problems. I always intended to pay the client back before anyone found out. That never happened. One bad decision led to another, and so began the long process of slavery, culminating in that time of confession. It took me seventeen years to reach the lowest point, to surrender all.

One of the most important things I wanted him to understand was my sole complicity in the business. I was thankful he believed no one had any knowledge or part in the criminality of BFG. Of course, they would have to do their due diligence and question my immediate family and assistant; but at the end of the day, they determined I acted alone. Aside from just not wanting anyone to know, I had to, at all costs, protect everyone from prosecution and keep them above reproach.

We were pretty much done talking, and he now knew everything. I was drained emotionally and physically. At that point, he left to go talk to his counterpart at the Securities and Exchange Commission (SEC) about the best way to proceed. The SEC is the federal arm with jurisdiction in these cases; however, because North Carolina has its own securities laws and had initiated the investigation, it also had jurisdiction.

While he was gone, he sent in a female agent to watch over me, so I was not left alone. I do not remember her name, but I remember she was a young black woman with a peaceful voice and smile. We talked casually, a simple "Hello, how are you doing?" kind of stuff. I found out she was a Christian during our brief time together. I remember thanking God for sending her. We talked about how relieved I felt confessing but how scared I was also. She said that I was going to be fine, that God had me in His hands and would take care of my family and me. I needed to hear that.

When Sean's boss returned, he said they had decided to share the case with the SEC, which really meant each agency would get a new notch in their belts for publicity and glory. He also said I was under arrest. This hit me like a proverbial Mack truck. I was stunned. I pointed out he had said several times that day I was *not* under arrest. Again, I was so naive about the judicial system. I guess I believed, stupidly, I could confess all this without an immediate consequence. I falsely believed he would continue to take all the evidence they came for and leave me a free man until some point in the future. I know, crazy thinking, right? That is exactly what I expected though. I expected some kind of consideration for the fact that I had come forward and was being honest. I still did not understand what being under arrest meant. After all, I had never been arrested before. I fully expected to be arrested at some point, just not right then.

There was lots of paperwork to do between the two agencies, the North Carolina secretary of state and the SEC. Proceeding meant me signing everything we owned over to the SEC. They would handle the receivership of all my assets, and North Carolina would handle the criminal prosecution. I did not have to do anything but sign my name. As much as I trusted this man, I believe he and the SEC took full advantage of my current weakened state of mind. At the same time, I wanted to do the right thing. I wanted no more to do with BFG, I wanted to show my willingness to cooperate, and it was important for me to show my children what it meant to step up as a Christian and accept full responsibility for my actions.

He came back when he had the paperwork ready to sign. He made it sound like these were standard arrangements for surrendering assets in cases like this. I was so exhausted by then; I was willing to agree to anything. However, looking back, for my family's best interest, I believe I should have refused to sign anything until I had an attorney. What they offered was inadequate, but in the inadequacy, God received great glory, as we had to rely on His provision fully. Looking back, I can see God's hand working to show His power and love for us. There has not been a single day He has not provided everything we have needed through our family and our brothers and sisters in Christ.

I signed the paperwork turning over everything we owned to the SEC. They were to provide $15,000 for my wife and allow her and our children to take their clothes and personal items from the house. With a stroke of a pen, I made them homeless and destitute. In less than a day, they went from believing they were very well off to having nothing.

Signing all that over was the easy part. Now came the hard part: telling my family. I called up to my parents' house and told Gilda they could come home. By this time, most of the agents were gone or were in the process of packing up and leaving. I was very nervous and crying nonstop. Gilda came in, and I was waiting for her in our bedroom. I hugged her tightly and said I had something to tell her. I was crying and trying to find the right words, but nothing was coming out. She held on to me and reaffirmed her love for me. She knew nothing about what I was doing with BFG. Finally, I was able to confess it all to her. She was such a rock of faith, such a godly woman. She did not yell at me, hit me, or do anything you would expect from someone who just found out they had lost everything; she held me, comforted me, reassured me she loved me, would never stop loving me, and would never leave me. Oh, how I needed to hear that!

You see, one of the lies Satan had me believing was that if I ever confessed, I would lose my family and they would all abandon me. I had no reason to think that would ever happen, and anyone who knows my family knows they would never do that. It is not in their nature. It is not what true Christians do. It is not what God does, and it is not what His Word teaches us to do. However, that is how confused my thinking was. My focus had gotten so far left of center that I fell prey to all kinds of twisted thinking.

Abandonment is a horrible thing. It is one of the hardest things to understand and deal with and one of the cruelest things to do to someone. I did not want to be abandoned. The thought of it scared me to death and was one of the most powerful forces that kept me bound to this sin for so long.

Jesus knows about abandonment. He was left abandoned in the garden of Gethsemane, by all his disciples. He was arrested, and all he saw were their backsides fleeing as fast as they could. Mark ran away so fast he left his clothes behind and ran away naked. Where were they during the night and the next day? His disciples were close by, some even within eyesight, but none were supportive. He understands our abandonments better than we do because He bore them for us on the cross. I do not think we realize that was a big part of what He carried away for us through the cross.

Gene Edwards, in his novel, *The Divine Romance*, writes from the perspective of angels about what was happening beyond the sight of a mortal man at the crucifixion. He tells how God the Father allowed the angels, this one time in their existence, the ability to transcend time and see from beginning to end what was really happening to Jesus on the cross. They could see the enormity of what was happening. They witnessed all sin, from the first sin by Adam and Eve to the last sin at the end of time when Satan was thrown into the lake of fire, being poured into Jesus. It was not just sin, but everything associated with it, including abandonment. Edwards describes the blackness and stench of every sin ever committed and yet to be committed being poured into Jesus.

I do not think we can fully understand what that was like for Christ, but I know what it felt like carrying my sin around for seventeen years. I also know what it felt like to finally give it up on November 7, 2008, to pour it into Jesus on the cross myself. We look at Jesus on the cross through the eyes of the Gospel writers, inspired by the Holy Spirit, and we think all the pain and agony Jesus is experiencing is from the physical beatings and the crucifixion process itself. That was the easy part for Him. That was nothing compared to having all, not just the sins of the day, but *all* sin for *all* time, past, present, and future being poured into Him. On top of all that, the eternal relationship Jesus had with the Father was at that moment forsaken. Jesus cries out loudly in Matthew 27:46, "My God, My God, why have You forsaken Me?"

There was no other way to reconcile us with God except for Jesus to carry our sins, and to do that, He had to also carry our abandonment from a Holy God who, because of His very nature, will not exist in eternity with sin. When God's Word states we have an advocate in Jesus, standing before the throne of God on our behalf, who has felt and experienced what it is like to carry the burden of sin on His back, we can take it to the bank. We can believe it, trust it, rely on it, be comforted and encouraged by it for all eternity. You can say, "No one knows abandonment like I know it," but you would be lying because Jesus knows, and He will never abandon you.

There was still more confessing to do. We called my parents, brothers, and pastor to come to our house. They already knew about the agents being there all day, but they had no clue about the bombshell I was about to lay on them. I really did not know how they would react. I knew how I hoped they would. They were all investors, and some of their extended family members and friends were also. My pastor's wife was my assistant.

After all the practice confessing I had done earlier, it was surprisingly easy to tell them. They had lots of questions. For obvious reasons, they were stunned, in shock, and numb. Their reactions were exactly what I had hoped for. They were very supportive of what I was doing. They are all godly people who understand and exhibit true, unconditional, godly agape love. They certainly were not happy about the situation or about losing hundreds of thousands of dollars, but they also knew the bigger picture of life, that material things are not important. We were all kind of numb initially. Having dealt with everything that was going on throughout the day, and also having knowledge of it all for the past seventeen years, I was probably the most lucid of the bunch. We stayed in the library for a long time, none of us wanting to leave. We all knew what was to happen next.

Finally, at about 11:00 p.m., Sean's boss came to say we needed to wrap things up and get going. I went upstairs to our bedroom to change clothes and use the bathroom. Gilda went along. When I was ready, we held each other tightly and cried together. I was scared of all the unknowns ahead, but at peace that I was not alone. Jesus was not only with me but also ahead of me. I was scared for my family, but at peace over them for the same reason. I was scared for the investors as well, but again, at peace over them for the same reason. Although it was too late to make the morning paper, it was sure to make the morning news broadcasts; and after the arrest, the Catawba County Sheriff's Department gossip lines would be ablaze. I hated for the investors to find out through any of these ways, but there was nothing I could do to change it.

As Gilda and I said our "I love yous," I told her there was a bag in the closet with cash inside. The agents had told her to take the kids and get out of town for a couple of weeks to avoid the firestorm and for their protection. They were not to tell anyone other than immediate family where they were going. We had two houses in Ocean Lakes Campground at Myrtle Beach, South Carolina. They told her it would be good for her to go there. I told her to take the cash and tell no one. I was concerned she would need it to survive. Of course, being the faithful, godly woman she was, she did not listen to me. Her cooler head prevailed, and she gave the money to the receiver, Walt Petit. We both agreed we did not want anything more from BFG. We both trusted God would lead and provide for our every need. We had to give up everything associated with that sin. I was very proud of her for giving up the money.

*****

Joshua, our oldest son, was on his way to meet up with some friends in Charleston, South Carolina, when Gilda called him and explained to him the events of the day. He was devastated. Instead of turning around to come home, he changed course and went to Myrtle Beach. Two of our closest friends lived there, Chris and Hannah. Chris was a pastor at a church near Myrtle Beach. They were introduced to us by our pastor, and we quickly became close friends. They were a young couple, less than ten years older than Joshua. Chris and Joshua were very close. They had been with us in Florida back in February when I received the call from William and had also accompanied us on a cruise to Alaska in August 2008. Joshua was going to their house until Gilda arrived at the beach.

Joshua was a senior business major at Appalachian State University in Boone, North Carolina. Part of the ever-increasing pressure, grief, remorse, and paranoia I felt was from the mounting difficulty of keeping everything from Joshua. It clearly appeared that BFG was a very successful business. I think everyone assumed Josh would come to work for me in the family business, but I could never have allowed that to happen. I told him he needed to get out and experience the real business world and become his own success, apart from me.

Emily, our oldest daughter, still lived at home, worked as a certified nurse assistant (CNA), and was planning her May 2009 wedding. Justin, her fiancé, came to the house that night. Emily could not leave town with her mother because of work and school, so she moved to my parents' house.

Emily took what was happening very hard. She and I used to love planning trips together. She, like all our children, was able to navigate easily through any airport or large city like New York or Washington, DC, at a young age. She and I especially enjoyed planning our trips to Disney World and Universal Studios. For her tenth birthday, she and I planned a weekend, father-daughter trip to the Mall of America. Em was my first child to love roller coasters and fast, scary theme park rides.

Hannah and Judge were twelve and ten years old respectively on November 7, 2008. They did not fully understand what was going on except that I was going to jail that night. As much as my heart hurt for everyone involved, it really was broken most for them, because they were so young. I had always held out hope—and even tried negotiating with God at times—to hold this inevitability off until all my children were fully grown. I know how important it is in a child's development to have a good family life with both parents in the home.

Hannah and I would have "Hanny days" when just she and I would do something fun together. It was not always something big. It might be as simple as getting ice cream together or going shopping or bowling. While I was at CCDC, she developed a love of coffee, and the first thing I thought when she told me was that there would be no "Hanny days" at Starbucks together.

Judge could not stand being disconnected from me every waking moment of his life. If I walked out of the house, within fifteen minutes and then about every hour or so until I returned, he would call me. He would say, "Dad, Dad, what are you doing?" I could always tell if he snuck away from his schoolwork and did not want his mom to know because he would be whispering into the phone. Then I would hear Gilda in the background calling his name, and he would say, "Gotta go. Bye!" He would then hurriedly hang up. There would be no more playing phone tag with Judge.

I am proud of the godly men and women my children have grown up to be. I can see how God has used this trial to make them into the successes they are today.

It was so hard to say goodbye, to let them go from my embrace. I had no choice. I had to be strong and not fall apart for them. They stayed in the house, and I left with Sean and his boss. They were very considerate of my family and did not handcuff me until we got to the car, out of sight of my family. That was the first of many times I would be shackled. It is a horrible feeling. You never get used to it. I remember feeling nauseous.

It is not a long ride to the CCDC, less than ten miles from my previous home. We spoke very little except for me giving them directions, which seems very ironic looking back. Other than crime shows on TV and being in prisons volunteering with Epiphany Prison Ministry, I had never seen the real inside of any kind of police station.

I was terrified, but I knew and felt the presence of God. I kept thinking of my family and how the victims would be affected when they heard the news the next day. I was so embarrassed for them as well as for myself. I knew the news would spread rapidly through the gossip lines. I also knew the bookkeeper and the insurance salesman would be laughing and gloating as they gladly said, "I told you so," to everyone.

When we arrived at CCDC, I was pretty much numb and exhausted. I am sure there were some important questions I needed to ask, but I was not thinking too clearly. I was just going through the motions. Looking back now, it was mostly a blur. This was a totally new experience, so I had no idea what to do or ask or say.

I remember it was around midnight. I went before the magistrate on duty. I was not sure if our close friend, who was a magistrate at the time, was working the night shift. Part of me hoped she would be and part of me did not. I did not really feel like confronting anyone I knew. However, it would have been nice because I would have trusted her to lead me in the right direction. I was given an extremely high bond, $1 million. None of the paperwork made any sense to me.

I later learned Sean and his boss requested the high bond because they considered me a flight risk. This meant they were afraid that if I were let go from custody, I might try to flee the country. I do remember thinking how absurd an idea that was. I was not that type of person, but looking back at the situation from their perspective, it was a wise assumption to make. They had to cover their bases. Although I had signed everything over to the SEC, the banks were closed by then, and I still had my passport. Bondsmen were always on call. If the bond had been set really low, I could have gotten out and left the country that night. For all they knew, I could have had money stashed all over the world. They had only met me that day, and even though they may have felt like they knew me well enough at that point to know I would not skip out, they had to play it safe. I had no knowledge of how bonds really worked or about how bondsmen did either. None of that was particularly important to me right then.

I remember being photographed for a mug shot and being fingerprinted. I felt so dirty and frequently nauseous. I do not remember who was doing all the paperwork, but I do remember everyone being kind. I am sure they could see the state of mind I was in. It had to be written all over my face. I was not their typical clientele, as I would learn over the next few hours. I was not drunk nor high, dirty, diseased, belligerent, or disrespectful.

The officer helping book me in told me he was going to put me in a single cell in one of the blocks in the old part of the jail. I thanked him, even though I had no clue what that meant. Before leaving the booking area, I was given a neon lime-green jumpsuit and shower shoes to wear. All my clothes were put in storage. I brought only my driver's license and my glasses from home. My license was put in storage, and I was allowed to keep my glasses. My feet were shackled, which seemed to serve no other purpose except to humiliate me. After all, you were in a secure facility with no way to get out. Every time you left the cell block, you were shackled. They were metal shackles, one around each ankle with an eighteen-inch chain connecting them. Even going a short distance, they would rub your ankles raw.

I was given a bed mat, blanket, sheet, toilet paper, towel, washcloth, and toiletries. I hobbled up a long ramp connecting the new part of the jail to the old. The old part was maybe thirty-five to forty years old and nasty. The hallways were fairly clean, but the cell blocks were nasty. The shower stalls were old and falling apart. They looked like a petri dish for every communicable disease imaginable. The cell I was assigned was right beside the showers.

I fell on the bed, exhausted. Finally, the emotions of the day hit me all at once, and I could feel myself falling into a deep depression. I lay there thinking about my wife, kids, family, friends, church, and all the BFG clients. I was not remotely concerned for myself, only for them. The depression was not about what would happen to me, but what would happen to all of them.

By the time I got to the cell, it was way past midnight, and I do not know what time I finally, out of pure exhaustion, fell asleep. When the doors opened sometime early the next morning, I stayed in bed. I could hear the other guys moving around in the dayroom walking by, looking in at me, talking about me. Obviously, none of them knew me, which seemed to surprise and confuse them. Apparently, the clientele at the jail were pretty much regulars from the various hoods around the county.

When breakfast came around, someone came by the cell and told me it was here. I ignored him, pretending to be asleep. I did not realize how big of a deal a simple meal was to these guys. A man could get killed over a meal tray. I heard someone say, "If he don't get up for lunch, we're gonna drag his ass out here and make him give us his tray."

I finally got up but still stayed in my cell. A couple of guys came by to get the 411 on the new guy. They were actually pretty friendly. I felt less afraid and more at ease after that and ventured out into the dayroom for a while. Of course, they were all curious about why I was there. It was pretty obvious I did not fit the norm. When lunch and supper came around, I gladly gave the trays away. I had no appetite. The food did not look too bad, but not too good either. It certainly was not what I was accustomed to eating. I did drink the Kool-Aid and tea though.

I was not in that block for more than a couple of days. Then I was moved to a two-man cell out in the main hallway going to the elevator that went up to the courtrooms. The decision to move me was twofold. One, for protection, because it was feared one of the victims might pay someone to kill me. Two, I later found out, was that I had been placed on suicide watch. Both things seemed ludicrous to me and more of just a publicity stunt by the sheriff's department and the district attorney. Although I was severely depressed—and anyone would be a liar if they said they had never thought about suicide when they were depressed—I would never have left my family to deal with all this mess. Also, I would never have given anyone the satisfaction of saying I took the coward's way out.

The only good thing about suicide would have been the insurance proceeds. I had a total of $20 million, but only half of that would have paid if I had committed suicide; the other half was not in force long enough to cover suicide yet. I am not sure how many victims would have known about that, but if they had, I am sure some would have been cheering for suicide. The insurance was very expensive, thousands of dollars in premiums per month, but I had taken it out over the years for two reasons: one was to provide for my family; the other was to provide for the clients. I also had $17 million on Gilda. Of course, the receiver for the SEC let it all lapse and cashed it in for what little value was left.

The two-man cell was better in some aspects than the single cell. Rather than having to deal with about twenty guys, I only had to deal with one at a time. It was also much quieter. The downside was being stuck in there with the same person for twenty-three hours a day. I was let out for one hour a day to shower and walk around in one of the blocks after everyone else was locked down for the evening. I had no choice who they put in the cell with me. I know it sounds terrible, but after a few days of observing the kind of people in jail, you start to wonder—is there this much inbreeding in Catawba County? It is really sad. The longer I was there, the more frustrated I became by the darkness that thrives in that place. Also, my heart broke for these people.

Those first few days and weeks I had numerous visitors. I do not recall them all, but their visits did help some with my depression. Just to be reminded of God's grace and love through others was a blessing and encouragement. Emily brought me one of her Bibles, a pocket version. That was my only possession those first couple of weeks. I would have killed should anyone have tried to take it. The fact that it was Em's made it even more valuable to me. I remember her future father-in-law came, a close friend from high school who is a pastor, a pastor from the church I grew up in, a pastor from my parents' church, and two pastors from my present church at the time. My wife, children, parents, and brothers also came.

The first day, a bondsman came to see me. He was very eager to help. I could see dollar signs in his eyes. I just laughed at him. For those who do not know how a bondsman works, they guarantee your bond to the court. In exchange, you pay them a nonrefundable fee of up to ten percent of the bond. As long as you show up for court, no problem. If you jump bail and do not show up, they have to make good on the guarantee and pay the bond to the court. Otherwise, it is just a line of credit. At 10 percent, that meant I would have had to pay him $100,000 to post the bond for me. There was no way I could pay anything, nor could any of my family. The only other option would be to put up property as collateral for the bond, but there was still a cash percentage that had to be paid to the court as well. It was beginning to sink in that there would be no way to make bond, so there was no way of going home anytime soon.

All the visits were video visits, not the face-to-face, in-person type. The only face-to-face visits were with attorneys and the receiver from the SEC. It would be more than fifteen months before I would get to see and touch my family again. Not being able to touch them was one of the hardest things to endure. We have always been a loving, hugging family. I knew from working with Epiphany Prison Ministry just how important the ability to show love and to physically touch another person was to an inmate. They told us it was one of the hardest parts of being in jail and prisons, but I never fully understood how that absence of touch could affect you mentally and emotionally.

The first roommate was no stranger to jail. He was a black man, maybe in his late thirties, who could not sit still. Because the cell was on the main hallway leading to the elevator going up to the courtrooms, there was a constant stream of shackled men and women going by our door, Monday through Friday. He knew almost all of them and had to get the 411 from each one, both going and coming. In the cell next to ours, they put a couple of women, lounge lizards, from one of the hoods in the county. Of course, he knew them too. The cells are connected by an air duct above the toilet and sink. He stood on the toilet and sink so he could talk to the women through the vent and watch them expose their breasts for him to see.

Fortunately, I did not have to stay in that cell for more than a few weeks. Then I was moved across the hall to a single, corner cell which was right next to the elevator and adjacent to a small four-man block. It was the captain of the jail who decided I needed to be more social. Because of this, I was moved back across the hall to another two-man cell.

One of my first roommates was a young man from a wealthy family. He had killed a drug dealer. He and I went each night to the same block to shower and use the phone. We became friends. He was related to some of my clients. When the captain found this out, he was moved across the hall to the single cell I had previously been in. It was funny, we could not be housed in the same cell, but we could go to a block together to shower and socialize and do Bible study.

The block we went to was a small two-man block with two single-bed cells, a small dayroom with a single shower stall, and a phone. The one constant occupant of one of the cells was Buck. He had been at the jail for over two years on a capital murder charge. All total, he would be there about four years while he waited for his trial. He was found not guilty. In the meantime, he was held without bond for nearly four years away from his children. Innocent until proven guilty? Ha! In today's justice system, you are often guilty until proven innocent.

Buck and Jon are both Christians. We did Bible study every night. Jon was eventually convicted and given about eight years, I think. Buck went home to his family. I have written to him several times but have since lost contact with him. I pray for him often.

When you are a Christian and willing, God will use you for His glory and to further His kingdom, wherever you are. I cannot remember a time in my life when I was not involved in some type of ministry. My God-given spiritual gifts are teaching, pastoring or shepherding, and administration. In every aspect of life, even during all those years of being a slave to the sin of BFG, God used His gifts in me to bring Himself glory. Jail was no different.

I tried every day to let His light and life shine through me. Being a witness for Christ is not always about preaching. Most of the time, it is about being willing and available. I did not have to initiate any conversations about Jesus. I just had to be patient and wait for whoever was my current roommate to ask questions. They would ask me about my situation, my family, or how I always seemed to be content, at peace, and smiling. Once they gave me an open-door invitation, I could explain it was all about Jesus and surrendering all to Him. They already knew I was a Christian by just watching my daily routines. I spent most of my waking hours reading and study-ing the Bible. Even the officers would ask how I could put up with the lunacy that surrounded me and still be smiling and at peace.

My whole life, I have been a smiling person. Many times, my face carried a smile that made me feel like a painted clown. It was not a true indication of how I felt, only a cover for how much I was hurt-ing. However, even in sorrow, we as Christians have so much to smile about. Once, I had a court appearance and was not looking forward to being in the public eye in a lime green jumpsuit with shackles on my ankles and my wrists shackled to my waist. The young deputy escorting me upstairs said to me, while sitting by my side in the courtroom, his grandmother said to tell me she was praying for me and my family. She also said to tell me she was "sorry we were being crucified by the media and on the internet." I remember silently saying a prayer of thanks for her, and of course, I had a smile on my face. The smile was because of God's love for me and the peace He had given me in that moment when I was feeling down. No one in the courtroom was in on the conversation between the deputy and me, or God and me; so to others, it looked like a smug, arrogant smirk. That is how it got blown out of proportion on the internet. It was also the picture that appeared in the next issue of the Hickory paper. My wife told me about it. When I explained what transpired, she said she knew the smile was one of peace in the Lord, as she sat praying for me as well.

One of my roommates was a very immature thirtysomething man, a true momma's boy, a spoiled brat. He was very emotionally unstable, cried a lot, and just wanted to go home to his parents, with whom he still lived. He had lived out on his own some, but basically lived his life as an irresponsible adolescent in a man's body. He too asked the usual questions, and I told him the same answer: Jesus. That was not the answer he wanted to hear. A few days later, same questions, followed by my same answer, followed by the same reaction. Finally, one day he asked again how I could be so at peace, but he ended his question with the disclaimer, "And don't tell me Jesus! I want some other way to be at peace!" I told him there was no other way. I do not know what became of him. He was moved to another part of the jail, and I never saw him again. C. S. Lewis wrote, "God cannot give us a happiness and peace apart from Himself because it is not there."

Another roommate was a young homosexual. He asked, I answered. However, he was different. He wanted to know more. One day he finally said to me he knew he could not be saved because he was gay. He had been told he could not be forgiven of his sins and was destined for hell. We worked through God's Word, walked the Romans road, through Paul's letter to the Romans, and showed him, we are all sinners deserving hell. I shared with him that thankfully, Jesus came to give us life. He cried huge tears as the love of Christ washed over him, and he prayed to receive the salvation of Christ. I do not know what happened to him either, but I know he understands that God loves all sinners and we are all imperfect in and of ourselves, but made perfect in Christ.

Another young drug addict in his early twenties moved in. He had some rough days going through withdrawal. We played lots of cards during the day when he was not sleeping fretfully or shaking and crying. He left to go to a drug rehab program.

One day, the door opened and revealed my next roommate, Greg. I knew Greg from high school as he was one year older than me. He worked for my dad's swimming pool business off and on for years before starting his own swimming pool repair business. Greg was severely depressed. He had really screwed up his life by drinking, partying, and cheating on his wife. She had kicked him out and divorced him. Because of his lifestyle choices, his daughter would not have anything to do with him. His wife had restraining orders against Greg, and he had been arrested for violating them. He realized how badly he had messed up his life, and he could see no way to set it right. He was trying but was not being very successful. He confided in me that he often contemplated suicide. I believed he could and would do it when he got out of jail. Greg was a Christian, and we spent many of the forty-eight hours he was there talking about God's Word and praying. He had a younger brother with AIDS and his elderly mother to take care of. Sadly, a year later, his brother and mother died in a house fire. I know the tragedy of this loss meant Greg had probably lost his will to live as well. Greg was found dead at his home less than a year later.

In the months following my incarceration, I got to know the guards pretty well. They all knew I was a different type of inmate. I did not cause trouble, did not curse at them, did not call them names, and did not threaten them and their families. I was polite and respectful. Some of the employees at the jail had known me and my family for many years. I was not given special treatment other than an occasional extra cup of coffee or meal tray. I was allowed most nights to stay over in the block with Buck to do Bible study for several hours. It was ironic. The captain would not let me move into the two-man block with Buck because it was too dangerous for me to live there with a murderer; however, it was safe enough for me to spend several hours alone with him each night doing Bible study. Again, I am certain that where I was housed was as much, if not more, about publicity and appearances as for safety.

*****

The first few weeks after my arrest, Gilda and my family had no success finding an attorney. No local attorney would touch my case because of the number of BFG clients who were victims of the Ponzi scheme. They did not want the negative publicity that went along with defending such a high-profile criminal. Plus, it was such a unique case; no one locally had the expertise to handle it. They branched out to surrounding counties and to references given by other attorneys, but still found no takers. It did not help that they had limited funds and were basically looking for an attorney to take the case pro bono.

After the story hit the papers and the TV, I received a note from one of the guards with an attorney's name on it from Charlotte. I thought, *Great, an ambulance chaser. Just what I need.* I kept the note in my Bible, just in case. Finally, after exhausting what seemed like all avenues, I gave the info to my wife. His name was Pete Anderson, and his partner was Will Turpening. They had seen my story in the media. Turns out they were not ambulance chasers, and this was the type of case they specialized in. Normally, for a case like this, their fee would have been in excess of $100,000. My family had less than $15,000 to offer them. They agreed to take the case, and when the money ran out, they petitioned the court to be assigned as my court-appointed attorneys. The court agreed.

Pete and Will were amazing. We initially met to get to know one another and for them to ask lots of questions. It was clear to us all that they were sent by God to help. There were so many things God did to show His love to us and His faithfulness to never leave us and to provide for our every need. The thing they did not know initially was that I had no intention of going to trial. I did not want to put any of my family or clients through that horrible experience, knowing what the outcome would be. Besides, I wanted to step up, take responsibility for the wrong, and be an example—a good example—of how a Christian should act in such a case.

The first few days at the jail, I met the receiver for the SEC. Walt Petit was his name. He was the guy tasked with collecting and liquidating all the assets and ultimately distributing what was left to the clients (after all expenses were paid). Pete and Will were not pleased I had met with anyone without being represented by legal counsel. However, after we talked and they understood my intentions, they were fine. They realized I would not be swayed from pleading guilty, straight up, to the crime, because it was the right thing to do. They never painted a rosy picture of any hope of not going to prison. Their goal was to get the best deal they could, to make sure, as much as possible, that I got a fair sentence. I had no idea this process would last for fifteen months, but then I had no idea how the system truly worked or, more accurately, did not work.

A date was set for a court appearance to enter a plea. I thought we were all on the same page. Expecting to walk in the courtroom, see Pete and Will, and enter a guilty plea, I was shocked to see a young female attorney I had never met. When asked by the judge how I wanted to plead, she stood up and entered a not guilty plea. I was stunned and speechless. I remember being angry and wanting to speak up and say, "No, I plead guilty!" I did not do this, though. God knew best, and He stayed my tongue. Afterward, she met with me and gave me a lesson in how this "song and dance" pony show worked. If we entered a guilty plea, we had neither options nor negotiating power. By entering a not guilty plea, we bought ourselves time and kept our options open. We could change the plea to guilty at any time. She explained Pete and Will were already committed to being somewhere else for another case and this first court appearance was just a formality anyway. I do not remember her name, but she was very competent and professional. I was impressed with her as well as with Pete and Will. My fears went away, and I realized how much at peace I was. I knew and felt God's sovereignty at work.

Some of my initial thoughts were for the clients, many of whom were in the courtroom every time I appeared. I knew how angry and stressed a not guilty plea would make them. I knew how the media would make it look and how the rumors would be flying through the grapevines and on the internet blogs and chat rooms. I was right. The worst for spreading rumors was the *Hickory Daily Record*, or more lovingly called throughout the Catawba Valley area, the *Hickory Daily Liar*. Several times, my attorneys had to confront them to have untruths removed from their websites.

It is unbelievable to me how much crap people will speculate and post on the internet, without ever stopping to think how stupid it sounds or makes them look. A couple of the funniest and most ludicrous reports were (1) I owned some heavy equipment (bulldozer, track hoe, Bobcat), and I was constantly digging holes on my property, so I must have money buried everywhere; and (2) I had traveled to the Bahamas and the Cayman Islands several times, taking big suitcases that never came back home with me, which must have been full of money. These are just two of the craziest, especially the travel one. Anyone who travels knows there is no way to travel with a suitcase full of money, because anywhere you go, you'll have to go through customs or airport security. Amazing! How can intelligent people believe these lies?

Sheriff's deputy Coy Reid, who later became sheriff, sat in on the first meeting I had with Walt Petit, the SEC receiver, and he asked if I had buried money on my property or took suitcases full of money to the Bahamas or Caymans. I actually laughed at him. I am not sure why he was even in that meeting, as nothing being discussed that day was of any concern to the sheriff's department. I am sure if I had had representation by then, he would not have been allowed in the meeting. In retrospect, if I had been thinking clearly at the time, I would have refused to meet with Mr. Reid there. At this point though, I wanted to be as helpful to Walt as I could. I did not want to hide anything. Walt was shocked at how cooperative my family and I were. He told me it was extremely unusual for anyone to cooperate. He quickly came to realize we were different. Another chance to be witnesses to the power of God in our lives and to the fact that because we are true Christians, not just church members—we are different. As the months wore on, my family continued to assist Walt.

With regards to Coy Reid, I do remember being uneasy with him being privy to any meetings. I did not trust the sheriff at the time, and I knew that anything Mr. Reid knew, the sheriff would soon know. I was not trying to hide anything, but I knew enough about the sheriff's behind-the-scenes political agendas to not trust him or his deputy. He and I had very different political views. I had supported his opponent in a Republican primary for a US House seat, which the sheriff lost.

Walt and I spent time that first meeting making a list of all the assets I could recall. He was appreciative of my help but was also very skeptical. I liked Walt for his professionalism and competent approach to his task. However, as the months and years dragged on, I (along with the complainants) became very disappointed with how the assets were liquidated. I do not think there were any assets that actually sold for market value. It was handled much like a fire sale. The main house sold for about one-fifth of its value, if even that much. The RV went for about two-thirds of its value. The other pieces of real estate and cars were the same. Over the last couple of years, I had started investing in art and had amassed over half a million dollars in paintings. The art sold for less than one-fourth of its value. There were Rembrandts, Salvador Dalis, Peter Maxes, Picassos, Chagalls, and more in the collection.

I loved collecting art! But my ultimate agenda with collecting it was to use it as an investment. I hoped it would be a valuable asset to be sold one day to help payback the clients. Additionally, I believed it would greatly increase in value over time. I was such a good client of the gallery I purchased most of it from that they flew me to Michigan to see a Dali decomposition they were trying to sell for $1 million. I cannot believe I was actually considering trading some of the collection I had for it. One of my building projects, which was nearing completion at the time of my arrest, was a new office. In that building, I had planned an art gallery to display the collection.

I became interested in collecting art on a cruise to the Caribbean with our pastor and his wife, my office assistant. They went to an art auction onboard the ship one afternoon and came back raving about how much fun it was and how much they learned about art history. The next day we all went, and I was hooked. I fell in love with Peter Max, Chagall, Rembrandt, and a few others. I bought over $100,000 of art. It was so much that we got invited to a tour of the bridge of the ship. Another time, we were invited to dine with the captain. Each time we cruised thereafter, the art auctions were a highlight of our trip. I look back on that and see so clearly how foolish it was. I see also that my motivation was not so much my love for art but for a possibility it could be a way out. The paranoia I felt about keeping up the appearance of being successful was also a deciding factor, probably more so than anything else.

My family was great to help make things go as smoothly for Walt as possible. My dad kept the yard mowed. One day, some of my family noticed some lights on in the house. My wife called Walt, and they discovered the house had been broken into. All the TVs were gone except two, as well as an autographed NFL jersey of Brett Favre. The TVs were all fifty-five-inch flat screens or bigger, and each worth $2,000 to $7,000. Ten of them were missing. They also stole a Mercedes S65 sedan. The sheriff's department tried to get Mercedes to track the car but they would not without my permission as the owner of record. They had to ask me for help. Of course, I did without hesitation. They let me call Mercedes and within thirty minutes, the car was located in Catawba County; the thieves were arrested. They had been going in and out of the house for two weeks at night. The TVs they sold on the street for $150 each, and they had been driving the car for two weeks. Some of the men in the gang lived only a half mile from the house. When they saw me in the hallway at the jail, they apologized for taking my stuff, as if that would help their case. I just laughed at them and thought how stupid they were. The stuff did not belong to me any longer. They just stole from the SEC, the federal government. That shut them up pretty quick when they realized they might be in even more trouble. I am not sure what happened to them. I occasionally run into an inmate who tells me he is a cousin or something to those guys. I have never asked what happened to them. I usually just try to avoid the conversation. Ironically, if they had not been greedy and taken the car, they probably would never have gotten caught.

*****

It did not take more than a few weeks for the lawsuits to start rolling in. I was surprised there were only four. One was from a man I had known my whole life. We grew up together in the same church; although he is a few years older than me, he may be one of the wealthiest landowners in Catawba County and holds a prominent position in county government. I certainly was not surprised he was suing me.

The second did not come as a surprise either. This couple was also lifelong friends from the church I grew up in. They are a few years older than my parents, and their children are a few years older than me. They were very bitter. It is sad the amount of energy we expend wallowing in our bitterness. We say we hate being the victim, but we work very hard to make sure that status is ever before our public eye. My heart breaks for this couple and their family. I want so much to make this right for them and all the victims, but I cannot give them peace. The peace they need only comes from Jesus, and they are hindering that by harboring bitterness and unforgiveness. I spend a lot of time praying for them.

The third did surprise me a little. It was from a couple who had been close friends for many years. The wife had been our doula coach for the birth of our last two children. We had served on numerous Via de Cristo, TEC, and Epiphany weekends together. I recently received a card from them after the passing of my wife of thirty-three years. They expressed to my wife how hard it had been to deal with all the hurt I had caused, but through the grace of God, they were able to forgive. They expressed their love for me and their forgiveness and the peace they have in the Lord.

The fourth was from an elderly couple who lost a lot of money and, I think, even had to sell their home to pay off some debts as a result of the losses. Again, I was not surprised by this lawsuit.

These were the only ones. I expected there to be many more. I had no intention of contesting anyone who would sue me. However, because these four did not just sue me, but also my wife and oldest son, who were completely innocent, we had to fight the suits. We had given everything to the SEC. Pete and Will told us they could not represent us in the civil suits and the criminal suits at the same time, so they recommended an attorney friend, Shawn Copeland. Shawn is not just a Christian in name or just on Sundays; he is the real deal. He lives his faith every day. He has, from day 1, represented us, knowing he may never be fully compensated this side of heaven.

The first time I met him at CCDC, the first thing he said to me was that my wife said I needed a hug, and he hugged me. He hugged me as I broke down and wept. I had told Gilda how much I needed some loving human contact. I had not been at CCDC all that long, but I quickly came to realize how much we need the agape love of God as expressed through the physical touch of another believer. As the saying goes, I did not know this man from Adam, and here he was holding me in his arms. I knew instantly he was not only an answer to prayer but was the hands of God reaching out to me, reassuring me, comforting me. After that hug, Shawn gave me his testimony and witnessed to me about God's love and reassured me of who I am in Christ.

He explained what was going on and what he was going to do. His strategy was to go before the federal judge and ask that all the lawsuits be placed in a sort of judicial limbo until the SEC finished with the sale and distribution of assets. If the judge agreed, the hope was at that point in the future, the litigants' attorneys would advise them there was nothing left that we owned worth suing for and would drop the suits. Pretty much that is what happened when it became obvious I would be in prison for a long time and there was no evidence to show my wife nor son were in any way guilty or involved. Eventually, they all dropped their lawsuits.

Shawn has been one of the greatest blessings our family has ever received from the Lord. He ended our first meeting by laying his hands on me and praying. Once again, God, through this faithful servant, lifted a great burden off my shoulders and gave me peace. Once I got settled at my first prison, Shawn came to visit me. He was not coming to take care of business, although we did take care of some paperwork that could have been handled through the mail. No, he drove over two hours just to visit with me.

God is faithful to His Word to never leave us nor forsake us. Many times, He shows His faithfulness through others. If you are feeling abandoned by God, maybe you need to step back and take stock of the people around you who may be God's way of showing Himself faithful to you.

When I was served the papers for the lawsuits, I remember immediately thinking of 1 Corinthians 6:1–11. Paul speaks to the Church at Corinth, and to us, about lawsuits against believers. He makes some very important points for us as believers and brothers in Christ. We are *in* the world but not *of* the world. We have a higher calling that is greater than the world. We are answerable to the One Who has overcome the world. Any disputes we have among ourselves, we are to handle *among ourselves* and with the help of the Church. We are not, for any reason, to go before a worldly court to settle our differences. I remember the first time I talked to Gilda after being served the papers, and she immediately said the same thing, referencing the same Scripture. We were not mad or upset at the people. We were heartbroken for them over being deceived by Satan into disobeying God's Word. We began praying for God to show them the truth of His Word and to lead them to obedience.

Another friend of ours, Bryce Thomas, works with the ministry Peacemakers. Bryce contacted the pastor at Saint John's Lutheran Church, where I grew up, about doing a conference for the victims at their facilities. He also contacted Gilda about helping us. Part of the ministry is individual counseling. He was not allowed into the jail to meet with me, but he began counseling Gilda to help her with all the emotions and people she had to deal with. He was a much-needed secure, private, sounding board for her. I still thank God for

Bryce and the ministry God has given him. He helps individuals, businesses, ministries, and churches understand forgiveness and how to embrace 1 Corinthians 6:1–11 and to settle their differences biblically. However, none of these people were willing to listen. He was also a great help to us when our church turned against us and forced us out.

After Gilda returned home from the house at Myrtle Beach, Todd, our pastor and close friend, came to see her at my parent's house. She told him how much she missed being in our church but did not want to cause any trouble or division. There were quite a few members who were clients of BFG. Although I had never purposely recruited business from church, they all came seeking me of their own free will. Gilda knew I was persona non grata. Todd told her without hesitation that she was welcome at church. He told her the Church is about love and forgiveness, and he would resign before he would let our church push our family away. Feeling relieved, she and the kids went back.

After several months, Todd called Gilda into his office for a meeting. He told her people were complaining she was being divisive, smug, arrogant, aloof, standoffish, etc. She asked him, "To whom?" She was trying to be low-key while at church, trying not to draw attention to herself. She also said she was giving those people who were clients their "space." Gilda did not want to cause them any undue stress or anxiety. She asked Todd to assist her in understanding exactly what she was doing to cause these feelings in people, and he could not give her any example. She left, not knowing what to do.

After some time passed, Todd called her into his office again. This time she was confronted by Todd and two deacons. They presented her with a document they wanted her to sign which stated she would stop being divisive in the church. Again, when she asked them to specifically state how, when, and to whom she had been divisive, they could not give an example. She asked to have a day to pray and talk to me. They refused and demanded she either sign it or she would not be allowed to return to the church. She signed it under duress and left feeling devastated. A short time later, she asked for a copy of the paper she had signed; Todd told her she could not have a copy. By this time, she was working through the pain and devastation with Bryce. As the Holy Spirit ministered to her, she was filled with the Lord's peace and strength. She and three of our children never returned to that church.

I was heartbroken by what our church had done to my family. They could have done anything to me, but not to my family. My family needed the Church to come alongside them and not only comfort but help protect and take care of them. I could not believe that some of my best friends there were not coming to their aid. This rejection, by the church we had poured our lives into over the past nine years, hurt me more than anything else up to that point. It was not so much that I hurt for us; I did greatly. However, I hurt for the church. Gilda and I prayed for the church. We prayed for God to forgive them and to move among His people there to bring repentance and revival. We prayed for Him to do whatever it took to draw the church back into a deep, intimate fellowship with Himself. We asked God to convict the soul of the church to not be "of the world" and to step up and do the right thing; to do the right thing by our family as well as by all the victims.

Over the last four or five years of BFG, business had been really good; lots of money was flowing in. I gave generously to many ministries, charities, and needy individuals. By far the biggest donations went to our church. The church was growing quickly and was making plans to build on. Over those years, I gave several hundred thousand dollars to the building fund, college ministry, and general fund. Money does strange things even to godly people. Greed is a terrible, debilitating sin. More than one church has fallen prey to it as well. I truly expected the church to willingly offer to give back all the money I had given to the building fund, at the very least. I was shocked they were fighting with the Receiver to keep the money.

I know many people blame me for the problems at our church that followed my arrest, but the problems were already there, festering below the surface. There were four pastors in ministry at the time; none of whom are still there. The senior pastor's marriage fell apart. There was infighting among the staff, the church stopped growing, and some of the ministries began to decline. Many wanted to blame me, and I took responsibility for my part, but the real downfall started over greed. My family and I were just the scapegoats. After my family stopped attending the church, the problems did not cease; they escalated.

We saw this as an answer to prayer. We were not praying for bad things to happen. We were not seeking revenge or the wrath of God. We were asking God to do whatever He had to do to rescue His people and restore them to Him. We loved these people as our own flesh and blood. Our hearts were broken.

I hurt for my wife and kids. I wanted to take care of them, but what could I do? I did the only thing I could: I prayed. I poured out my heart and feelings to God. He showed me He was faithful, all-powerful, and sovereign over everything. He was removing everything in our lives that was a crutch or hindrance to us fully and completely relying on Him. He took everything, and we were left with only Him. Gradually, as we were ready, He began to restore, and He always provided.

First, our family needed shelter, and my parents generously provided their home for my wife and kids. My parents moved into a one-bedroom apartment next door and allowed my family to live in their home. They have provided for their transportation and many of their living expenses. My son's business has been successful, and he provided many things for his mom and siblings. My wife had many Christian sisters through her many years spent in Bible Study Fellowship (BSF), who came alongside her to help. When our church abandoned us, my brother's church, New Life Authentic Christian Community, took my family in with open arms. We joined New Life in 2009.

I received a letter in November 2011 from the chairman of the deacons of our former church. He informed me I was being excommunicated. I wrote him a lengthy reply and left the door open for them to respond. That was the last I heard from them.

God brought two friends of ours, Paula and Ruth, back into our lives to support Gilda. They would come to the house and spend time with her, supporting her with unconditional love and friendship. They were a safe haven for Gilda. This is another example of God's faithfulness and steadfast love for us.

Gilda needed a job. The $15,000 given to her by the SEC, which she did not receive until several months after my arrest, was not going to last the three of them very long. We still wanted to homeschool our children, so whatever she decided to do for income would have to allow for time to do school. She was encouraged by one of our sisters-in-law to take the class to become a substitute teacher for Catawba County Schools. This seemed to be a great option. She filled out all the paperwork, attended the class, and began substituting at Claremont Elementary School. The teachers were very kind and supportive of her and said she did an excellent job. Apparently, some people began complaining to the school system administration and the board of education members. The attorney for the system called her and told her she could no longer substitute; they felt she was a security risk because my criminal case was a high-profile case. The principal at Claremont School stood up for her, telling his bosses she was doing an excellent job. He did so to no avail. Now what? Another disappointment, another door shut in her face because of me. My wife was so amazing. As much as this hurt, and as many tears as we shed before the Lord, we still had unbelievable peace and love for these people, no bitterness. We saw it as another opportunity to praise and wait on the Lord to provide, and He did.

Gilda began working for herself, cleaning homes, and in the summer doing swimming pool care. God was faithful in bringing good, generous people for her to work for. It gave her a way to provide for them and allowed her to homeschool, help take care of her aging mother, and work with various ministries in the church. She did not make a lot of money. In fact, she could be considered, by our country's standards, to be below the poverty level. Indeed, without the help of our family providing housing, she would not have been able to survive without going on welfare.

Extreme times like these are when you find out who your real friends are and how deep your friendships really are. I look back and see so clearly how many friendships were grounded only in the wealth they thought I had. I lost all but a handful of friends, and I gained some new ones I will cherish forever. Some friends I considered my closest, most intimate, best ones were so devastated and felt totally betrayed. They bought into all the rumors and false reporting, and they completely ended our relationships. I cannot say I blame them for having any of these feelings, but not one even bothered to contact me in any way to ascertain the truth or to reach out in Christian love to try to rebuke, restore, or reconcile. As Christian siblings, we are supposed to reach out with agape love for one another, regardless of the other person's actions. In this case, I had no way to reach out to them from jail. I do hold this against them; they did not even try to reach out to me. A true friend would have tried.

God was faithful and provided people to be His emissaries. One of the dearest was Martha. I have known Martha my whole life. She is a member of the church I grew up in. Within a few weeks following my arrest, she began sending me cards. This continued weekly for fifteen months. She was always so loving and encouraging; never judgmental.

Cris, another one of my good friends, a classmate and friend from high school, started visiting me every Friday at the CCDC. He and his family are some of our dearest friends; they have stood by us through everything. Cris and my times together in visits always centered around God's Word and what I was studying that week. Cris always allowed me the time to let go and express my feelings and emotions.

Eric, a pastor at my parents' church, began visiting every few weeks. Our visits were different than with Cris. It is hard to explain, but even the visits with Cris, being as open as they were; it seemed without knowing it I was still not opening up all of what I was feeling. When Eric would come, God would use him and his questions to move me to pour out my heart even more. I came to cherish the visits with these two men as much as my visits with my family.

Scott, the pastor at the church I grew up in, came regularly to the jail. His visits seemed to be God's way of always keeping before me His agape love and to uplift me and encourage me. Pastor Steve from our new church came regularly, and it seemed to me God was using him to say, "You are still a part of the Body of Christ."

Pastor Jeff, from my former church, came in the beginning, but then stopped. I can only assume church leadership made him stop because of the ongoing battle with the receiver over returning the money. I missed Jeff's visits and would have liked for them to have continued.

Once a week, a group of Christian men came to the jail to witness and pray with the inmates. One of them was Roy. He always brought his old magazines to share. One of those magazines was *Israel My Glory*, published by Friends of Israel. This became one of my favorite magazines to read. Roy and I became instant friends. I eagerly awaited his visits each week. His pastor was also very supportive of my family and me. He shared his life story of being responsible for an auto accident as a young college student in which his friend was killed. He shared with me his struggle with guilt and forgiveness. His witness really helped and comforted me as I struggled with both guilt and forgiveness as well.

The days at the jail went quickly by, but as the one-year mark approached, I was becoming increasingly impatient. During those days, I was consuming God's Word. While at CCDC, I read His Word in total four times in fifteen months. Every day, I would begin with a Psalm, a chapter of Proverbs, a daily devotion from *Our Daily Bread*, and usually, I would read fifteen or more chapters of Scripture. I divided my time by reading and studying three books of the Old Testament then two books of the New Testament. I also had some fiction and nonfiction books to read. However, it was getting time to move on.

The weekends and holidays were the worst at CCDC, because the courts were not in session. This was a bad thing because to keep peace in the blocks, the guards would put a "boombox" radio in the hallway and blast it so everyone could hear it. Usually, the most central place was near my door. It was not so bad on Sundays; I could talk them into putting it on 106.9 WMIT, which is Billy Graham's Christian station from Black Mountain, North Carolina. Even then, the "demons" would become very agitated after a short while and start complaining until the guards turned it to Power 98, or as they called it, Nigger 98. That has got to be a station that is straight out of hell. Every second or third song was the same one played over and over. You know the one I am talking about. It is the one that is blasting from the car next to you at the stoplight, vibrating your teeth. Yes, that one! Every weekend, every holiday, all day long! I told my attorneys I wanted to sue the jail for cruel and unusual punishment. They laughed, but I was serious. It was torture, and it was driving me crazy. Locked in that little room all day, having no way to block out the loud noise of that constant tune, was enough to drive any sane person mad.

What was taking so long, you ask? If you want to plead guilty, you just have to have a sentencing hearing and be done with it. It seems simple, right? No, not so simple. The wheels of justice do not turn that fast. Remember that we are playing a political game. Everyone who is an elected official is in this game, has a stake, a political agenda. They want to protect and exploit for their own benefit. The list can get quite long—district attorney, state attorney general, judges, sheriff, secretary of state, and on and on. Even from my side, the attorneys were playing the game to make sure I got the best opportunity for a fair sentencing.

It did not take long for DA Gaither's and Sheriff Huffman's (no relation) political agendas to make themselves known. One day my attorneys came to me to report on their latest meeting with DA Gaither. They so wanted to take this guy on in court, not because they thought they could get me off scot-free, but because they said the district attorney was so incompetent that they would enjoy the game of making him look like the idiot he was.

Normally, this is how the system works: You are charged with a crime. The district attorney decides on behalf of the state whether or not to offer you a plea deal for a lesser charge or a certain amount of prison time in exchange for a guilty plea. If you take the deal, you go before the judge, who usually accepts the deal on behalf of the state, and it is official. Most of the time, you and the district attorney may go back and forth, rejecting pleas until the district attorney comes with a final offer. This supposedly saves the courts lots of time and money by avoiding jury trials.

Pete and Will came to me that day, early on, and asked, "What have you done to piss these people off?" To which I replied, "I don't know. I don't trust them. I don't like them. The only thing I can think would have to do with politics." They both smiled. "Tell us more." I explained to them about supporting US congressman Patrick McHenry, in the primary and general elections. In the primary, he was opposing Sheriff Huffman, so I was opposing the "good ole boy" system in Catawba County. I shared with them my wife, and I had become good friends with the congressman. We attended and participated in his campaign events in Catawba County. We also hosted events in our home to garner support for him. We were close enough to the congressman that he took time in 2007 while we were in Washington to take us on a personal behind-the-scenes tour of the Capitol building, along with a trip through the private tunnel connecting the House office building to the Capitol. I told them about my local involvement with politics and how I was constantly opposing and exposing corruptions in our local government. Now their meeting with the district attorney was making more sense to them.

DA Gaither made sure there was no one except my attorney, Pete, and himself in the meeting, so he could easily claim, if this proposal went south in a handbasket, the evil JV and his attorneys made it up. There would be no witness to what was offered. DA Gaither was not offering any official plea deal except a thirty-year prison sentence. If I did not take this one-and-only offer and if, once at trial, by some miracle I received less than thirty years, then he would just keep bringing new charges and going back to court until he got his thirty-year sentence. Having quietly said this, he had a "but" coming, an exception. However, if I could provide him and Sheriff Huffman information of any wrongdoing by *any* public official I had supported with regard to campaign finances, then he would be willing to negotiate for a lesser prison term.

When Pete and Will told me this, I just laughed. I told them DA Gaither was referring to the US congressman. I explained to them that the congressman, as far as I knew, was one of the most honest and trustworthy persons ever to serve in the US House of Representatives. Even if I wanted to, I could not give the district attorney what he wanted, because it would be a lie, so they went back and told him, "No deal." This was fairly early in 2009.

Pete and Will wanted to hold out and planned to go to court when our most favorable judge would be in our district. They also liked messing with the district attorney's mind. He was beginning to doubt the likelihood of his success in court against Pete and Will, who have quite the reputation in cases like this. He kept up appearances to the media and the victims that he was in full control and confident of the outcome. However, I do not know how many people in those two groups actually know this, but he had gone to the North Carolina attorney general and told him he would rather he do the prosecution than himself. This would take the heat and responsibility off him. That way, he could still relish in the glory of the outcome or pass the blame off to his "higher-ups" if things went badly for the state.

About that time, we decided to change my plea to guilty. Immediately, DA Gaither took the case back from the attorney general because now he wanted all the glory for himself since there was a guarantee of a prison sentence. Pete and Will thought we had the most favorable judge we were going to get. Plus, I was tired of jail life. I was ready to move on. I wanted this to be settled for my family and for the victims.

It would still be weeks before we could go before the judge for a sentencing hearing. During that time, the young attorney Pete and Will had assigned to me months prior, Luke (not his real name), had been preparing everything to be presented to the judge on my behalf. This included letters, character witnesses, history of my community service, etc.

Luke, I found out in one of our first meetings, was not a Christian. I had some things I wanted to discuss with him at one of our meetings, and I sensed he was not a believer. This made a difference in his being able to understand where I was coming from. I asked him, point-blank, if he was a Christian, and he told me no. I do not remember what it was I wanted to talk about, but I believe the point was God wanted me to know how to begin praying for Luke, more than He wanted us to discuss whatever it was I had on my list.

I began to pray for Luke's soul and tried to be a witness to him every chance I had about God's power, love, and grace in my life. I tried to do this without beating him over the head with the Bible. I also enlisted my family to pray for Luke. I still pray for him. I have not had any contact with him since the hearing, so I do not know if he has accepted Christ as his Savior, but I sleep easier knowing I was faithful to God's calling to witness to him. Please pray for him as well. It matters not that his name is not Luke, because obviously, God knows who he is, so please pray for his salvation. I hope one day to meet up with him again to find out what God has done in his life.

Luke is one of the many people I have met in my life whom I do not want to go to heaven without. I do not remember where exactly or who first asked the question of me, but I remember it was a preacher. He was talking about having a burning passion to evangelize the world. To make his point of the desire we should have for all lost souls, he asked, "Who do you not want to go to heaven without?" That question hit me square in the face. Ever since, I have looked at people from that perspective.

I remember being depressed early on at CCDC over all the pain so many people were experiencing because of me. I would pray fervently for God to just "come quickly." I knew if He returned, all the believers who were suffering would be taken up to meet Him in the sky, and this would all be over for them. That group would have included most of the victims. I prayed this every day.

God is so great, amazing, and full of wisdom. He knew my heart, and why I wanted everyone's pain to end. He knew how much my heart broke for them. He also knew my heart for wanting my own pain to end. The prayer, although a virtuous prayer, was also a selfish prayer.

One of my greatest pains stemmed from not being able to care for my family in all aspects—physical, emotional, and spiritual. I spent countless hours crying out to God for my family. One day, God spoke to my heart distinctly. As I expressed my struggle with holding onto Him and my family simultaneously from my position, I felt an overwhelming peace. The Holy Spirit revealed that I was attempting something only God could accomplish. The words of Jesus in Matthew 10:37–39 echoed in my mind: "Whoever loves father or mother more than Me is not worthy of Me, and whoever loves son or daughter more than Me is not worthy of Me. Whoever finds his life will lose it, and whoever loses his life for My sake will find it." I sensed Him saying, "You have to let them go. You're clinging to Me with one hand and to them with the other. You lack the strength to do both. I am strong enough. Release them and grasp Me with both hands. Trust Me to care for them." I humbled myself before Jesus and entrusted them to His omnipotent hands.

Yet I continued to pray for His swift return. In a letter, my wife mentioned discussing salvation with Judge, our youngest, who was ill. Despite understanding the significance of committing his heart to Jesus, Judge wasn't ready. Reading this, I recognized the folly and self-ishness of my prayers. Judge was at the age of accountability to God for accepting or rejecting the gift of salvation. I panicked, wishing to retract my "come quickly" prayer. But I knew God understands our hearts beyond our words. He knows to interpret our true intentions, even when our prayers seem foolish.

This realization profoundly impacted me, especially consider-ing the potential consequences for Judge should Jesus return immi-nently. He would be left alone at eleven years old in a world devoid of believers. Although God would never abandon him, the thought of my son facing such isolation terrified me. This experience trans-formed my approach to prayer. I will never again pray for Jesus to "come quickly," so long as there are those I cannot bear to enter heaven without.

Selfishly, I want Jesus to return this very minute and take His Church to be with Him. Unselfishly, what I pray now is for Him not to come until every soul that will accept His free gift of salvation has heard the gospel of Jesus Christ and accepted Him as their Lord and Savior.

Judge has since given his heart to Jesus, and I rejoice that if Jesus comes today, my whole family will be with Him. Yet my heart still breaks for those who will be left behind. I do not believe there will be many children left behind, but there will be some who have been given the chance to accept His gift and decide to wait or outright refuse it.

I pray all the time for the victims of my crime. I pray for God to look out for them, to provide for their needs, physically, emotionally, and spiritually. I pray for Him to give them peace and freedom and a heart of forgiveness. Of the hundreds I pray for, there are two in particular that I pray for very specifically. They are two people I definitely do not want to go to heaven without. Let us call them Barry and Glenda. Please join me in prayer for their souls. I do not know if it is fair to say they are two of the bitterest victims, but they have been the most public and vocal.

Most of the victims preferred to stay out of the limelight and chose not to talk to the media, recognizing how untrustworthy it is and not wanting their involvement broadcasted and printed for the world to see. However, Barry and Glenda were different. We all know the kind of victims they are. They love reading about themselves and being quoted in the papers, and they record for posterity every newscast on which they are interviewed. They are the kind of victims the media have on speed dial and whose home addresses are stored in the media's GPS. They never failed to be quoted and interviewed every time I went to court or every time there was a news release from the receiver. They personify the perfect people the media love to exploit. Typically, they engage their mouths long before engaging their brains as they pontificate for the cameras. The quote I read from them that broke my heart for their souls was something to the effect of, "We hope he burns in hell and we hope we get there first so we can light the flames for him."

I cannot say for sure whether or not they are saved; that is something only God knows, but based on their quote, I have serious doubts. I truly want Barry and Glenda to be in heaven with me. Please join me in prayer for their souls and for their peace and forgiveness. I desire to be reconciled with them someday, as I do with all the victims.

*****

The day was fast approaching for my sentencing hearing. In the weeks prior, Pete and Will explained how it would typically play out and that I needed to prepare my statement to the victims and the judge. They wanted me to write it all out and let them edit it. I could not do it that way. I tried. I made an outline of things I wanted to say, but I was at total peace that God wanted me to speak from my heart and not read a prepared statement. Pete and Will were not happy about it, but they knew my heart and went along with me on this. I have always been a good public speaker, so I was not concerned. I had my list. I practiced over and over every day, and each time it came out different. I was not worried about it. I was at peace and so very ready for this part to be over for myself and everyone else.

The day finally came—January 25, 2010. The officer came to my cell to get me. We started toward the elevator, and I asked if I was not supposed to change into "innocent" clothes first? The answer was no, and I asked if he was sure. I was pretty certain I had a suit and tie somewhere. Same reply, no. We were proceeding down the hall behind the courtrooms when we met the sheriff coming around the corner. He took one look at me and accosted the officer, "Why in the hell is he not dressed? Get him back downstairs and get him dressed!" To which I simply looked at the officer and said, "I told you so."

Before going into the courtroom, I met with the judge to go through the court documents, which basically say I understand what is about to happen and I have made this decision of my own free will without any coercion. Looking back now, the attitude and demeanor of the judge was the first indicator that all of it was just for show, and the final outcome had already been decided before ever getting this far. It didn't dawn on me then, but I just had a weird feeling about it.

I walked into the court for the first time in "innocent" clothes and unshackled. In Catawba County, you enter from behind the judge's bench, so you are facing the entire courtroom. As I walked in, I noticed the courtroom was packed. We had asked for the judge not to allow cameras but were denied. This was a big political event for all the elected officials, and they wanted all the mileage they could get. I did not really care about the media coverage for myself, but I knew my wife, kids, and family would be there. In fact, my wife was to give a statement. I really did not want any of them to be exploited by the media.

Still, I look back, and I see God was running the show and nothing that happened was ever out of His control. What those in charge allowed for their own gain, God allowed because so much of what happened was a witness to His love, grace, and forgiveness. This was a day I had bathed in prayer for over a year. The first time in my daily Bible study routine I read Proverbs 21:1, "The king's heart is a stream of water in the hand of the Lord; He turns it wherever He will," I began praying that verse for the judge. I did not know until right near the end, who he or she would be, but I did know he or she needed to be covered in prayer. I prayed for God to turn the judge's heart, not to my favor, but to fulfill His will and ultimately bring about His glory. I prayed for us to be all we could be for Him. I wanted the world to see Jesus at work in our lives that day. I prayed God would use us to reach out and touch whomever He wanted with His grace, love, and healing.

I walked in and sat next to Pete. I was not nervous or anxious. I felt kind of numb to it all; maybe it was just the peace of the Lord. Maybe it was just a totally new experience, and I did not really know what to feel. I did not look at anyone specifically in the crowd of a few hundred. It would have been nice to see my family sitting close, on the bench behind me, but I knew they would be near the rear to make a quick exit to avoid the media.

The assistant district attorney began with a character assassination. I remember thinking, *How can they say these things about my character without ever knowing me or talking to me?* We all do things that are completely out of our character at times. He was not even trying to present a true picture of who I am, but then, that is really not his job. His job is to present a case that will sway the judge to his side and to impose the greatest punishment possible. He wanted to further his career and his office.

It was interesting that the district attorney, Mr. Gaither, was not handling this himself. I believe partly because he was afraid to go up against Pete. Also, by assigning the hearing to his assistant district attorney, Mr. Bellas, he could hedge his bets in case things did not go his way. In that event, he could pass blame to his underling. He also could not know fully that our intentions were not to try and present any type of defense, only to present the truth, uncolored.

In the process of his character assassination, he was focusing on my Christian background. It seemed pretty clear to me, he had no understanding of what true Christianity was ever about. Throughout the hearing, he made numerous statements which I believed were intended to scoff at Christianity. However, I would have to agree with him that my sin was certainly not consistent with what God desires of His children.

It takes only one sin to discredit us before a holy, perfect God who plainly states in Romans 3:23, "For all have sinned and fall short of the glory of God, and are justified by His grace as a gift, through the redemption that is in Christ Jesus." Therefore, if we were to look at every person to have ever lived on the earth, save Jesus, there is not one worthy on their own to be called righteous. Yet that is what Mr. Bellas was painting out to the court. He was saying I was not worthy to be called a Christian, could not be a Christian, and in fact, had used Christianity only as a cover to deceive.

I remember talking about the day's events to my wife on the phone that evening. It was a testimony to how attuned to one another and to God we were, because almost simultaneously we both began commenting on Mr. Bellas. When he began his tirade against Christianity, we both at that moment, began praying for his soul. Nothing else seemed important at that instance in court except his soul. It was as if God literally said to both of us, "Pray for him *now!*"

Mr. Bellas was referring to some photos of my vehicles during his character assassination, pointing out to the judge a Christian bumper sticker on the rear bumper of "my BMW." This immediately caught my attention for two reasons. One, I did not own a BMW. Two, I hate all bumper stickers and would never have allowed one on any of my vehicles. I asked Pete to let me see the photos. Right away, I understood Mr. Bellas's error.

I was arrested on Friday. On Thursday, I had taken a barbecue grill up to Marion Correctional Institution to let the prison ministry, Kairos, use it for the weekend. When I got there, I found out they also needed my truck as well. My friend, Glenn, loaned me his

BMW and agreed to return my truck the following week. The BMW Mr. Bellas had the photo of and that the district attorney assumed, without checking the registration, was mine because it was in my driveway actually belonged to Glenn.

I pointed this out to Pete, who immediately pointed this out to the judge. I was surprised by the lackadaisical attitude of the judge concerning this error. It was just brushed off as unimportant, but to me, it was a big deal. This was my character Mr. Bellas was destroying, my faith he was mocking, and ultimately my Lord. I began to realize at that point the day's proceedings were merely a formality and had no bearing on the outcome. It was an attitude of, "Are you seriously going to make a fuss over such a minute, unimportant error in the grand scheme of things? Sit down and shut up while we go through the motions for the media. None of this really matters in the court's decision anyway." That is how it came across to me.

Mr. Bellas continued for what seemed like forever. I sat listening but not really listening as I kept praying for him. Then he made a comment about being a good friend with one of the victims. My ears perked up then. During the six years I served on the Catawba County Board of Education and the years on the Catawba County Board of Adjustments, I learned a great deal about the term *recusal.* To *recuse oneself* when serving in a legal capacity or as a public official means if you have a personal involvement somehow and there could be reasonable doubt as to your ability to be fair, then you remove yourself from the proceedings. After hearing Mr. Bellas's comment about being friends with one of the victims, I thought certainly the judge or Pete would step in. I had decided not to intervene but to test my theory that nothing said was of any importance to the outcome and see what happened. Nothing was said by anyone. Later, I asked Pete about it. He explained to me it was okay for the assistant district attorney to be friends with the victims, and this did not present a conflict of interest. Had it been the judge, then it certainly would have been a huge problem. He agreed it was very unprofessional on Mr. Bellas's part to point out his friendship, but not illegal.

After the assistant district attorney had his say, it was Pete's turn. He presented my case very well, pointing out my life history of community, church, and family involvement. He refuted some of the things Mr. Bellas had said. He called forth Cris Alley and my wife as character witnesses. I had not seen my wife in the flesh for fifteen months. I wanted to go to her and hold her during her testimony. We smiled at each other. My eyes filled with tears. When Mr. Bellas had his turn to question Gilda, he tried his best to discredit me more by trying to get her to speak against me. He prodded her as to her continued commitment to our marriage. I was so proud of her. Our commitment to our marriage has never been an issue for either of us. She emphatically stated our vows were "until death do us part," nothing else. We enjoyed being married for thirty-three years, four months, and twenty-three days, until God took Gilda home. She presented a testimony of God's agape love for us and of His and her full unconditional forgiveness for me.

Cris stated his opinion, as an ordained minister and as someone with firsthand weekly knowledge of my spiritual condition, regarding my understanding of what I had done and my unwavering commitment to take responsibility to do the right thing. They both gave witness to my remorse and tried to give an accurate picture of how any of us could be caught up in and enslaved by sin in our lives and how none of us are immune to the power of temptation.

During the hearing, the agents for the secretary of state's office testified as well as the receiver. Both stated how amazed they were with my cooperation during the last fifteen months. They stated this was unheard of. They were equally amazed by my family's cooperation as well.

This had been a long day. After lunch, the victims were allowed to speak through what are called victim impact statements. Of the hundreds of victims, only a few chose to speak, but many chose to write letters to the court. One of the administrative assistants from the district attorney's office read some of the letters. Of the ones who spoke, their statements told of their disappointment in me, how they knew me and my family, how they hurt, and what their losses meant to them. Some were very kind and stated their forgiveness. Others were very bitter and angry.

I did very well throughout the day, emotionally keeping it together, until the victims started speaking. This was the hardest part of the whole hearing. I wept at each one. I made a point to keep eye contact with each one, hoping to convey with my eyes what I was feeling in my heart. I wished I could go to each one to offer my personal apology.

The final item on the agenda before sentencing was my statement to the victims and the court. Although I was openly weeping, I was at ease and at peace. My statement was one of explanation, not excuses; one of remorse and apology, not begging for mercy. By this point, I had placed all my fears and worries before the Lord and rested in His hands.

All throughout the hearing, I had been closely watching the judge, aware of his actions at the bench, his reactions, or lack thereof, to things said. His demeanor was one of boredom, of impatience, as a man who had more important things to do and was counting the minutes until this was all over and he could get on with his life. He made notes, shuffled papers, did busy work as though he were multitasking on many things at once, rather than paying attention to the proceedings before him. Again, I noted how all this seemed not to matter to the outcome decided beforehand.

When it was all over and time for the judge's part of the hearing, he did not hesitate. He did not take any recess while he considered my fate. He immediately said for me to rise, and he stated that because of the severity of the crime in which I stole the life savings of the victims, many of whom, he stated, took thirty or more years to accumulate, he was sentencing me to a thirty-year minimum prison term.

When he said that, there was a collective gasp in the filled courtroom. I do not think anyone expected that long of a sentence; although, the district attorney was not visibly surprised. Obviously, he knew what was coming.

I do not remember reacting at all. I think many thought I would break down or pass out. I did not have any reaction, other than to be glad and relieved it was all finally over. Afterward, downstairs in the storage room where I was changing out of my suit, a couple of the deputies were with me and talking. They asked how I was doing. I expressed my relief and my peace of heart. They said they could not believe how much time the judge had given me. They expected twelve to fifteen years but never thirty. They thought it was excessive.

I guess I had already prepared myself for such an outcome. I was so focused on getting this part behind me, and thankful for the little bit of closure this would bring the victims. I was also focused on my family and what they might be going through having to leave the courtroom and face the media. The deputies could not believe how calm I was, and how I could have a smile on my face. It was another opportunity to give God the glory He warrants from us in every part of our lives.

*****

I have had much time since that day to ponder what happened and to analyze the amount of time. I know there are those bitter victims who would agree with Barry and Glenda that it was not enough. However, there are also those who understand sin, forgiveness, grace, and mercy, and who would equally argue it was excessive. Initially, I was on both sides of the fence. Now after careful analysis, I would say it was excessive. I would like to make my case for why.

I had twenty-eight charges for obtaining property by false pretense and securities fraud. I could have been charged with two charges for each account holder, which would have been a possibility of about a thousand charges. This was how the district attorney tried to make it sound that he was doing me a favor by only charging me with twenty-eight. With twenty-eight charges, and the possibility of having been given sixty to eighty-one months for each, running consecutively, would potentially be 1,680–2,268 months or 140–189 years. I should be glad to have only gotten 30 to 40 ½ years, right? I am sure that is how the judge saw it as well. This was turning out to be one of the easiest feathers in the caps of both the district attorney and the judge that they could use in their future campaign propaganda. Interestingly, it was indeed used that way.

I know every election following my sentencing that the district attorney dropped my name repeatedly. He wanted to make it look like he was saving the day. In reality, he did nothing more than preside over a hearing where he never spoke, and I believe the outcome was already decided before the bailiff said "All rise." He did most of his talking to the media and to the victims, both in private and one on one. He also had met with the victims corporately after each court appearance.

But hey, that is how politics works. I know this from my many years of playing that game myself. The general public has no inkling of the amount of corruption that goes on behind the political scenes. It is even at the board of education level I was serving in. I was shocked at all the scandals and corruption I encountered during the six years I served.

When it came time for the sentencing phase of the hearing, the judge stated, because I had stolen the life savings of the victims, which had taken them thirty years to accumulate, he was sentencing me to a thirty-year minimum sentence. At first hearing, that sounds fair. I thought so, and I am sure some of the victims, especially the angry, bitter ones, thought so too. However, let's look at it in more depth, from another perspective. Suppose there had been only one victim and one charge, and suppose Judge Bell applied the same logic, that I deserved a sentence equal to the amount of time they took to accumulate their lost investment. Here is where his logic and the law fall apart.

Per the sentencing guidelines, for one charge, the most I could be sentenced to is sixty to eighty-one months, not thirty to forty and a half years. It would appear then, by his logic, the law is unfair to the victim. In which case, the judge would claim his hands were tied by the law, thus taking the heat off him when the victims began to call foul. But in that instance, there would be only one victim and one "voter" instead of hundreds of victims and hundreds of "voters."

What the law does allow is for the judge, "at his discretion," to run the sentences *concurrently*, meaning "all together as one," or *consecutively*, meaning "one after the other." Judge Bell chose a combination of the two in order to accomplish his objective. He ran six sentences consecutive and twenty-two concurrent. Nothing wrong with that—it is all legal—but is it *just* and *fair*? Again, some, especially the bitter victims, would say yes, while many more would say no. Why the difference in opinion?

I would put before you, it really comes down to a true understanding of God's Word. He says, through Paul, to the Romans in Romans 12:19, "Beloved, never avenge yourselves, but leave it to the wrath of God. For it is written, 'Vengeance is mine. I will repay,' says the Lord." It kind of sounds like He is saying we do not need the law and sentencing guidelines for punishment. We should leave it all up to the Lord. However, that is not the case. Our laws and sentencing guidelines are what help to keep our society civilized and curb anarchy and chaos. They are good and serve society well when applied properly with wisdom and impartiality. We need a court system to apply wisdom and impartiality because if left up to those who have been wronged, there would most often be none; vengeance would almost always prevail. Whether we understand punishment and vengeance as two different things entirely or not is where the two different opinions come from.

A godly understanding of this truth leads us to see punishment as just and fair, which says sixty to eighty-one months is sufficient for stealing something that took thirty years to accumulate. If we claim the punishment is not justified and fair, we have to ask, what is our motivation in making such a determination? I would put it before you that in most cases, the motivation is revenge.

Now from the judge's perspective, what would be his motivation to want to give more than the required sixty to eighty-one months? His motivation is most likely not first and foremost revenge, but political gain and possibly revenge to a lesser degree. I am not totally faulting the judge; after all, we are all human, and it would be impossible to not be influenced by our fallen human nature. That is why God says to leave the vengeance to Him, because He is the only one who can be completely fair, just, and impartial. Only a perfect, righteous, holy God could handle vengeance without messing it up. We cannot.

It is also why I believe it is unfair to allow a judge to have unlimited discretion with regards to running sentences consecutively. I believe they should have discretion, but it should be limited. It is impossible to completely remove the influence of political gain and revenge from the system, but it is possible to remove the tools with which to act upon these influences. For example, in North Carolina, a judge cannot run more than three misdemeanor charges consecutively, regardless of the crime and number of charges, but with felonies, it is unlimited. You cannot tell me district attorneys and judges do not analyze every decision they make and consider its implications in the next election. There is no way that does not happen. They are human. They could not stop it even if they wanted to. I am not saying they are incapable of making the right decisions without succumbing to that influence, but the temptation is there. Limits placed on them by the statutes and sentencing guidelines should serve as checks and balances against the abuse of the power given them by the people.

Judge Bell's logic for choosing thirty years is flawed as well. He had no way of knowing, by any of the evidence shown in court, how true his statement about the victims having worked a lifetime to accumulate or earn the investment they lost really was. For all we knew, they may have won the lottery. I am not denying some may have taken a long time, but certainly not all. Again, even then the law only allows for sixty to eighty-one months punishment.

I think it is highly suspect that Judge Bell took no time in deliberation of the sentence, and the fact that the district attorney made it clear he would accept no less than thirty years, it certainly appears there was some behind-the-scenes deal making going on, some possible conspiracy to further both political careers.

The other perspective to consider is the overall fairness to the public. Is the sentence one that serves the greater good of society? Is society safer because of a thirty-year sentence? Would society be just as well served by a five-year sentence? I have been involved in politics long enough to know politicians' general view of the voting public is one of feeble-minded patsies. What is really sad—it is a true assessment. It matters not your education level or income level, how up-to-date you are with the latest news, polls, op-eds, or social media outlets; if you have bought into the rhetoric you are safer because of longer sentences and bursting-at-the-seams prisons and jails, then you qualify for this general political view.

The public wants the criminals off the streets. I agree 100 percent. How we accomplish that goal is where we differ. "Out of sight, out of mind" works great for both the public and the politicians. The public only wants to know the problem of crime is dealt with; they do not care how it is done or how much it costs, as long as they do not have to deal with it. "Make us safe at all costs." The politicians are happy to oblige and ride that sentiment all the way to reelection.

I can hear it being said now, "He is just bitter because he is sitting in prison for thirty years. He should have thought about that before he committed the crime." I admit, there was a time I would have felt that way. Yes, now I have a different perspective, but none of that changes the fact. The fact is, it costs the taxpayers in North Carolina approximately $30,000 per inmate per year. With approximately thirty thousand inmates, that is a yearly cost of $900 million, give or take. I wonder how supportive of Judge Bell's decision or the district attorney's handling of my case the public would have been, if, in their campaign ads, they not only used my name as an example of how they made the streets of North Carolina safer, but they also pointed out how they, on their own, decided to spend a million of your tax dollars to lock up a man for thirty years who is clearly not a threat to the physical safety of society?

There are alternatives for punishment that would serve the victims better than long prison sentences. Cal Thomas—a popular nationally syndicated columnist, speaker, bestselling author, political analyst, and radio host—addressed this very thing in 1993. In his column, where he was referring to the sentence given to Jim Bakker, he said, "Perhaps Bakker should not have been sentenced to prison. He was a nonviolent, not dangerous offender and there are already too many of them being warehoused expensively in federal and state institutions. They take up space that could be used for those who are serious threats to the public." He goes on to say of an alternative: "Restitution and community service for Jim Bakker and for many white-collar criminals would be far preferable to several years in prison. The public interest is not served by continuing Jim Bakker's incarceration… Jim Bakker could have a greater influence outside than in prison… The parole commission should let Jim Bakker go, and the occasion should be used to begin an examination of the entire federal prison system, preferably before the 'tough on crime' demagoguery of the next election cycle begins. It's long past time to renovate the way we handle non-violent, non-dangerous offenders" (Thomas 1993). This was 1993 when he said these things, and it has taken the last five years that Congress has begun to overhaul the federal system. The states are even slower to respond, and North Carolina has always prided itself on being one of the toughest when it comes to prison sentences. And where has it gotten us? Overcrowded prisons and jails, no reduction in recidivism, and escalating costs.

An aside: I find it interesting that Jim Bakker was invited to attend, along with family and friends, the funeral of Reverend Billy Graham.

Which better serves the public and the victims in my case, a thirty-year sentence at an estimated cost of $1 million or a five-year sentence and a lifetime of working to make restitution? It is really a no-brainer. Restitution is not something new. Even in ancient biblical times, they understood this concept. If you were sued by someone and could not pay or refused to pay, you were sent to debtors' prison, where you remained and worked until you paid off your debt.

Here is another thought. It is kind of a slap in the face to the victims to give a sentence so long where there is no hope of ever getting restitution for their loss, and on top of that, requiring them to pay taxes to feed, house, protect, clothe, and provide healthcare for the man who caused their loss. And the whole time in court and in the media, they are applauding the district attorney, the judge, and the system. They even voted them back into office. Do you still think I am wrong about my assessment of how politicians view the general public? That whole "tough on crime" rhetoric is job security for these people.

I can sense there will be some reading this who still disagree. I am okay with that and respect your opinion. Let me make an analogy to help make this more personal. We all tend to agree the national debt is a huge problem, and we would all like to see it go away. However, we have accepted it as a forever-necessary evil of the world we live in. We recognize it is out there, but it is, for the most part, out of sight and pretty much out of mind on an everyday basis. We tolerate it and do not really worry about it too much. Otherwise, we would be more proactive in doing something about it. It is just not too personal for the average voting American.

Suppose the people holding all that debt, our nation's creditors, decided to place liens on every American's property, all of it, and you could not sell anything without paying your share of the debt immediately, right off the top? Then how passionate would you be in demanding our elected leaders do something about it? It would all of a sudden become very personal.

What I am talking about is essentially the same thing. What if your line item for state taxes on your payroll statement was itemized to show how much *you* are spending on prisons, education, roads, parks, salaries, and everything else? Would it maybe change how you vote?

In North Carolina, our public school teachers have historically ranked near the bottom of the pay scale in the country. How much money could be moved from the prisons and jails budgets to education if we really took a serious look at what we are doing with regard to nonviolent, nondangerous felons and long sentences?

When considering sentencing, how do you factor in and quantify what is enough? Punishment is whatever form is payment for a wrong done. The victims lost millions of dollars. How do you repay that equitably in punishment?

Judge Bell chose to quantify my punishment into time—thirty years, to be exact! But what will be the actual cost that I will pay? The victims lost material possessions, money. They suffered great emotional loss as well. I am not making light of that fact, and that can never be fully repaid. It sounds trite, but at some point in our lives, we have to choose to let that hurt go, to nail it to the cross of Christ.

Not only have the victims suffered, but so have I! I have lost the blessing of time. I have given up time with my children as they are all now adults. I missed all four of my children's weddings, their birthdays, and the milestones of their lives. I have missed the births of my grandchildren and the small events that surround watching their growth. I have given up precious time spent with my parents and siblings. But the greatest loss was not being able to support my wife through some of the most heart-wrenching and painful challenges that life levied upon her. Through her valiant battle with cancer that ultimately cost her life, I was not there to comfort her, to hold her hand in those final moments. I was not able to dry her tears or ever again embrace her.

How do you quantify all that? When does all that add up to punishment? Money is something that can be replaced. These are moments never to be recovered!

One of the first questions we have to ask is "What exactly is the purpose or goal we hope to accomplish with prisons anyway?" Prisons should serve three purposes: public protection, rehabilitation, and punishment—in that order.

The prime purpose of any prison system is public protection. We understand this to mean, when someone is a threat to the safety of society as a whole, or an individual or a group in society, that person should be isolated in a controlled environment away from those he or she wants to harm. This is a no-brainer. In this sense, prison is just a warehouse.

The secondary purpose should be rehabilitation, which is a word I detest. I detest it because it is a fallacy. It just does not work in its present form. I am not saying it is not a great goal, but it is nothing more than a bill of goods being sold to the voting public—and the elected officials who control the purse strings—by the Department of Public Safety (DPS). It is a propaganda vehicle to maintain the funding for the DPS and provide job security.

What I have seen of the DPS's efforts to "rehabilitate" inmates is a joke. There are some valuable classes offered, and the inmates who choose to participate do learn some valuable skills. There are a few certifications such as diesel mechanics, barbering, HVAC, culinary school, etc. that are all good. However, even those are worthless unless you significantly change inmates' lives. Classes such as Life

Skills, Thinking for a Change (CBI), and Character Traits, as well as twelve-step programs such as Alcoholics Anonymous (AA) and Narcotics Anonymous (NA) are often ineffective. The one program that had the potential to make the most progress in this area was completely cut a few years ago to save money—the chaplaincy program. The chaplaincy program became a community-funded program.

The overall tone, goals, and ultimate success of any organization is set by management. People will for the most part, do and act exactly how they are expected to with the proper motivation and leadership. I was told once, by an upper management employee of the prison system, all inmates were the lowest scum of the earth; and if I did not like what he had to say, I could go ahead and write all the grievances I wanted. They were not worth the paper they were written on, and who would the officials in Raleigh believe anyway? Would they believe me, one of the lowest scums of the earth, or him, a trusted management employee? This man is not only still in prison management but is also one of the instructors for staff across the state prison system.

You know what? He was only two-thirds right. Grievances, for the most part, are not worth the paper they are written on, and I would believe that way more than 90 percent of the time, the officials in Raleigh do not believe the inmate. However, he was one-third wrong. Inmates are not the lowest scum of the earth. They have as much value in God's kingdom as anyone, including this prison official. Only God can change the inmates' lives, not a self-help program or vocational skill. Prison will change anyone's life, but not in a positive way. Only Jesus Christ will make everyone who comes to Him a new creation. That is a 100 percent success rate. Why would we try anything else with a lower success rate?

Recently the Department of Justice (DOJ) sent experts to study Germany's prison system, as reported by *USA Today* in 2015. It seems Germany had the same philosophy the US has today, only back in the 1960s. They were parking people away in prisons, letting them out after long or short sentences, only to "welcome" them back shortly thereafter. They decided to change their philosophy and got serious about rehabilitation and doing things that seriously impact inmates' lives. Now decades later, their prison numbers are significantly lower, and their rate of recidivism is one of the lowest in the world. Their per capita crime rate is, as well. Their streets are relatively safer than in the US.

Had I been sentenced under the US federal system, the mean length of sentence in months per offense in 2019 was twenty-two months, with the median length being twelve months. That translates to 132 months for six consecutive sentences or eleven years, as opposed to thirty years in North Carolina. I would be a free man by now in the federal system. Instead, I am not even halfway through my sentence in North Carolina.

*****

The first prison I was assigned to had a wooden sign posted at the intake area where you got off the transport bus. It said "The Rock." As you got off the bus and proceeded through a line of guards, they were all pointing at the sign, smiling and saying, "Welcome to the Rock. Get used to it."

Fear, resentment, bitterness, psychological abuse, paranoia, etc. are not successful rehabilitation strategies, yet that is what North Carolina and the majority of other states and federal governments have been about with their prison systems. They have all focused on the third purpose, punishment. The powers that be believe wrongly that by extreme punishment, you achieve rehabilitation. Make someone miserable enough, and they will straighten up and live right in order not to have to return to prison. Well, wakeup call! That has proven itself futile! Unless they significantly change their whole life, unless they become a "new creation," they are doomed by the current system and society to become repeat offenders and career inmates.

Like Germany, where it has taken decades to change their philosophy, it will be a very time-consuming change in the US as well. Only changing the justice system and its philosophy will not do it. Society's philosophy toward inmates must change also. In most cases, inmates will not be your best employee, but they can become one of your best. They will require society's investment of all its resources to accomplish the goal, but it can be done. It can, to a much lesser degree and at a greater expense, be done without the Church's help. However, with the Church in partnership with the justice system and society, the changes can be astounding.

If we were to assign degrees of blame for our failure to inmates, the Church would have to be at the top of that list. The Church so often quotes the Scripture, Matthew 25:36–40, where Jesus teaches that when we visit those in prison, we are doing it to Him. The Church uses it to pat itself on the back when it goes into the jails and prisons for Bible studies, worship services, and Christmas meals. The Church says, "We are doing the work of the Lord," and that is very true.

Inmates, like all lost souls and children of God, need to hear the Word taught and proclaimed. The Great Commission in Matthew 28:19–20 gives three directives: make disciples, baptize, and teach them to obey. I believe the Church has falsely convinced itself it is fulfilling the Great Commission in prisons when, in fact, it is only fulfilling one part, the baptizing part. This is the salvation component of the Great Commission. Matthew writes, "Baptizing in the name of the Father and of the Son and of the Holy Spirit." Do not misunderstand me. I am not saying baptism saves, and I am not going to get into that whole doctrinal debate. However, of the three legs of the Great Commission, baptism is the one which speaks to sharing the Good News of Jesus Christ's work to save us. I am also *not* saying the Church should stop what it is doing in our prisons.

What I am saying is we, as the Church, are neglecting the other two pieces of the Great Commission, making disciples and teaching to obey. These are also essential parts to fulfilling God's call to us. They are also the most difficult, time-consuming, and costly of the three. This point can be summarized with one word: *mentoring*. God calls all of us to both be mentors and to be mentored.

What do we know about mentoring someone? One, it is very time-consuming if it is done correctly. Two, it is very physically, emotionally, and spiritually draining if it is done correctly. Three, it can be very expensive at times if it is done correctly. Four, it is one of the most rewarding experiences for the mentor and the mentored if it is done correctly.

What is the recurring theme in these four points? "If it is done correctly." Doing anything *right* is never easy—*never*! Let us look at a familiar parable Jesus told in Luke 10:25–37. This is the parable of the Good Samaritan. The story in a nutshell is, a man is walking down the road, gets beat up, robbed and left for dead. A priest passes by, but does not help followed by a Levite who does the same. Only the Samaritan steps forward and provides the help.

There are so many lessons in this story, but I want to expound on the costs of getting involved in someone's life in a life-altering way. Had the man been sitting by the road having lunch when the priest came along, and asked him to preach a sermon on the benefits of keeping the Sabbath, the priest would most likely have stopped and done so. Had the traveler asked the Levite to share benefits of serving in the temple, he most likely would have done so. The man's immediate need was not for a sermon or a Bible study. He did not care how much these passersby knew until he knew how much they cared. His needs could not be met in the short term or cheaply. He needed someone who could climb down in the ditch where he lay among the refuse, dying in his afflictions. He needed a Samaritan willing to tear his own clothes into strips for bandages, a Samaritan willing to put this filthy, bloody, naked man in his clean, new car, and take him to a hotel, and out of his own pocket pay for his room, board and anything else he needed until he returned. He needed a Samaritan willing to put aside his own schedule because the traveler had more important needs. Which of the three—priest, Levite, or Samaritan—had an impact on the traveler in a positive, life-altering way? Which of the three is the traveler most likely to listen to a gospel message from? Sometimes we have to go to the places we least want to go, alter our schedules, give up our time, and reach deep into our pockets in order to fulfill the Great Commission.

I hear some of you saying, "Everything run by the government does not want the Church's help." That is a poor excuse that will not stand up to scrutiny when we are presenting an account of our lives before the Lord. The Church has pretty much been kicked out of public schools, but we have not given up on education. To fulfill the Great Commission, the Church owns hospitals, shelters, schools, soup kitchens, food pantries, clothing closets, and orphanages. Why does the Church not own any prisons? I know there are some good church-run programs to help inmates when they get out of prison, but they are woefully inadequate, underfunded, and understaffed. Besides that, they are too little too late. They are at the wrong end of the process. The best time to make an impact on inmates is while they are serving their sentences.

I hear the naysaying already. "That will never work. The government will never provide funding for a privately run Christian prison." I say, where there is a will there's a way; if the will is God's, there is no stopping it. After all, He owns all the resources. If it were a ministry of the Church, it should not be funded by the government, but by God's people. The work of the Church is the responsibility of God's people to fund. We are to be in the world, not of the world. Which brings God the most glory: a mediocre ministry in the jails and prisons once a week or month, or a ministry so big that only God could bring it to fruition?

The third purpose of prison is punishment. Punishment is important. It is important for justice and fairness. It is also important to God. He tells us in His Word what we sow we will also reap, and that our actions have consequences. We have to be held responsible for our actions.

If we want to be a good parent to our children, we need to follow God's guidance of not sparing the rod. God, being the perfect parent, does not spare the rod from us as His children. He does not spare us from punishment because it is good for us. The key is to administer the punishment in the correct amount and the correct way. For example, a spanking to a child is good, while a black and blue beating is not. One is correct punishment, the other is abuse.

Prison can be the correct punishment, or it can be abuse. I am not speaking again about the length of sentences. I have already made the point of how that can be correct or an abuse of power. Here I am speaking about *how* the punishment of prison is administered. Prison will never be a pleasant experience, nor should it be. However, it should be an experience that makes an impact on your life in a positive way, not a negative way.

That being said, I am surrounded every day by men who seem to love prison. It is one big party for them. It is a necessary part of living the life they love on the street. It is safer and healthier for them than living on the street. When they have served their time, they will go back to the same lifestyle that sent them to prison. Within a year, they will most likely return to do more time. Their friends and family members are often in prison, so they get to hang with their homies. I refer to them as career inmates. I tell them all the time, "Prison is like Motel 6. We will keep the light on for you."

The thing is, they don't really love prison. What they love is sinning. They love sinning so much they are willing to give up a huge part of their lives for prison in order to return to the sins they love. That is why recidivism will remain so high, until you completely change their lives from the inside out, making them a new creation. The only way to do that is through Jesus.

The lifestyle they lived on the street may, on the surface, seem fun to them, but if they were truly honest with themselves, that lifestyle is unsafe, even deadly, miserable, wrought with disease and illness. Their life expectancy probably doubled when they came to prison and will be cut by half when they are released. Deep down, subconsciously, they know this to be true, and I believe this is one of the reasons they keep coming back. These guys may be clean of drugs and sober for the first time in years. They realize the dangers of all that stuff, but if you ask them what they plan to do when they get out, they answer "Drugs and alcohol." Yet in the same breath they will declare they are done coming to prison.

They come to prison and are clothed, warmly housed, fed three meals a day, have round-the-clock health care, all utilities paid for, have no rent, and have cable TV. Many of them have families that send them $45 each week to spend on junk food and drugs that are available everywhere and that allow them to gamble on every kind of sports event and card games. The government—or rather you, the taxpayer—care for their multiple children by multiple "baby mommas." They have it made compared to their life on the street. They never have to worry about their neighbor shooting them.

Do not misunderstand. Prison is still a very dangerous place. People still get beat up, stabbed, cut, raped, robbed, etc. every day in prison, but for the most part, it is much safer for them than being on the street.

Prison undermines and furthers the destruction of already dysfunctional families, if you can even call them that. Children of inmates are multiple times more likely to go to prison than children of noninmates. Marriages rarely survive any prison sentence; this is mostly because they are already headed for destruction, and prison was just the nail in the coffin. The only ones that survive are those that were on solid biblical ground from the beginning, which are pretty much none.

There is currently no consideration given to how the inmate's punishment affects their family, yet it is also the family's punishment. Granted, in many cases, the families are better off and in less danger without the inmate present; however, the sad reality is the absence of one bad influence is quickly replaced by another.

I am fortunate to have great, godly family members who have stepped up and filled the void left by my absence. Still, it is not the same as having a father or a husband present. They can only take up so much slack for me.

I remember early on in my time at the CCDC, and even up to the present, feeling the pain, loss, and guilt of not being there for my family. I know firsthand how divorced men feel when they only have a few hours on a weekend to spend with their children. It is all but impossible to be a good father with only a few fifteen-minute phone calls and one two-hour visit per week. The prison system does nothing to help families stay together and there are those who argue it is not the system's responsibility. Again, it comes back to the overall philosophy about the end result you are looking to accomplish, and I would say the real responsibility lies with the Church.

*****

About a week after my sentencing, I left CCDC headed for processing at Central Prison (CP) in Raleigh, North Carolina. It was a cold morning in the middle of a winter storm. I was traveling shackled in the back of a paddy wagon–type van with two officers up front. I thought, *I've been here fifteen months and you choose to transport me on one of the worst winter weather advisories of the year.* In spite of that, we made it to CP without any problems. I was actually glad to finally be leaving CCDC, but I was also very nervous and apprehensive. I had no clue what to expect. I had very few possessions to take with me—only a few legal papers, cards, photos, and my special Bible. Everything else, I left with my friend Buck.

I was the only one going through intake that day. This was fine with me. I really did not want to be sitting all day going through the process with a room full of guys. The whole thing was surprisingly easy. They searched my possessions, strip-searched me, and gave me clothes, bedding, and toiletries.

CP was a hodgepodge of buildings, ranging from many decades old to a new hospital unit under construction at that time. I was led down what seemed like miles of hallways to the processing units; these units were all the way at the end of one building in the old death row section. The blocks in this section consisted of sixteen single cells, each with a bunk, locker, and stainless steel toilet-sink combination. There were eight cells each on two levels, two showers, and a dayroom with tables and a TV. There were a number of these blocks on two levels in this section. This would be my "home" for the next month while I went through processing into the system. I had numerous medical examinations, mental evaluations, drug tests, questionnaires, and photos for my ID card.

Every survey and questionnaire was obviously developed with the career inmate in mind. I was answering one drug questionnaire that consisted of multiple-choice questions about my drug use. I pointed out to the examiner that I could not answer any of the questions because there was not an appropriate answer for not ever having used drugs. He did not know how to respond except to say that if I had ever taken an aspirin, then I had used drugs and had to answer the questions accordingly.

Inmates still to this day cannot understand how I have lived my whole life and never used drugs nor abused alcohol. They also cannot believe I have been married to only one woman, and all my children have the same mother. The whole idea is foreign to them. They all say, "You don't belong here." To which I always reply, "I know. I deserve to be here, but I do not belong here. Thanks for noticing."

I was very nervous at first but quickly realized the men in my block were not going to beat me up, rape me, or kill me. They were actually quite nice and helpful. Most of them were career inmates who knew the procedures already and could answer my many questions. Two other guys were there for the first time like me. When we were not at some examination or meeting, we played cards and watched TV and slept to pass the time. Everyone was at different stages of processing. Every Tuesday and Thursday, the buses ran to transfer inmates all over the state, so there was constant turnover. As soon as a cell was vacated, someone else moved in.

I had the corner cell, which had two outside walls that leaked when it rained. The bed was along the outside wall. It was so cold I could see my breath. I filled six Coke bottles with hot water to help stay warm in bed. I wore thermals all the time, but I still froze. Fortunately, I was only there for one month.

*****

The day I left started off very early at 3:00 a.m. There was a full bus leaving that day. We were processed out, our possessions searched, and we were searched. We were on the bus by 6:00 a.m. All buses across the state meet at one location to swap inmates and then return to their home bases.

I already knew from my case manager that I was going to a medium custody facility, but I did not know where I was going. During the course of one meeting, she made the comment that she did not know why, with the amount of time I had, I was not going to close custody. She said that never happens; I should be going to close custody for at least a few years. I smiled to myself and said a prayer of thanks to God. She did not understand how it happened, but I did.

While processing out of CP, they told us where we were headed. I had hoped to be going west, close to home, but instead I went east to Tabor City Correctional Institution (TCCI). TCCI was near Wilmington, along the South Carolina border, less than an hour from Myrtle Beach, South Carolina.

TCCI opened in 2008, so it was only two years old when I arrived in March of 2010. It is a huge place with twenty-four blocks, four stories tall, housing as many as 1,500 inmates. It was a nice, comfortable facility, but it was managed by very cruel people. You could feel the darkness upon arrival. The hatred oozed out of the people, both staff and inmates. I knew it was an evil place as soon as I got off the bus, saw "The Rock" sign, and heard the taunts by the officers.

By the time I finished going through their processing, I had been on the "bus trip from hell" for twelve hours and had only slept three hours in the last thirty-six hours. Yet God continued to watch over me. I was housed in the kitchen block. Each block housed over ninety inmates in the medium custody part of the prison. My first roommate was a great guy. He went by the name Super Dave. Most inmates go by some nickname, which may have something to do with where they are from, like New York or Philly, or something to do with their personality, like Joker or Player. If you are more mature in age, you might be referred to as Old School. I stuck with JV, but guys also called me TA (Teacher Assistant), Teacher, or Preacher. The officers referred to you by your bed number or last name.

Super Dave was great. He had been in prison for nine years and knew all the ropes. He was an excellent chess player and worked in the kitchen. I was thankful for his guidance.

Immediately, I put in a request for a job in education. I was there about two months when a TA position came open in the Adult Basic Education (ABE) class. I was called down to interview with the teacher. She was thrilled to have someone with my educational background. She was a very nice lady and was good at her job. She taught the ABE class, which was the elementary grade level. TCCI had three levels of GED classes: ABE, Intermediate, and GED. She was a nice-looking lady in her early fifties, a divorced cougar, and proud of it. She loved younger men, no one over thirty. She was not interested in any serious relationships or in any of the inmates, but she was hot on the trail of several young officers. Many of the inmates in her class purposely failed the advancement tests to stay in her class.

It is really sickening the way inmates view and treat women. If I were a woman, there is no way I would work in a prison. It matters not how old you are, what size you are, or how ugly you are. The majority of inmates will fantasize and discuss among themselves how they want to use and abuse you. If you do not go home every day feeling as though you need an acid shower to scrub the filth off from being raped all day long in the inmates' minds, there is something wrong. That is the way they were brought up to view women. They have no respect for women.

I have also seen women working in prison who thrive on the attention, and I have seen women and men fired for having sex with inmates. I have seen some get fired for bringing in contraband such as tobacco, drugs, alcohol, or cell phones to sell to inmates. Then there are those women who work in prisons because they hate men and thrive on the position of power they have here.

Thankfully, all these people are the minority of staff in most prisons. Most staff members are good people, men and women alike. Many are Christians and see their job as a ministry. Still, many of the good ones also hate their job. It garners little respect both on and off the clock. The average starting pay is approximately $30,000. Employee morale and loyalty are probably among the lowest of any industry. Most work another job on their days off to survive. Why do they stay? People covet the state's health care and retirement benefits so much that they are willing to spend thirty years of their lives being miserable in order to get them.

I am thankful for the people who work in prisons, all of them. I spend a lot of time in prayer for them and their families. I am always respectful to them and do all I can do to let them know I appreciate what they do.

*****

It has been interesting to see how inmates and staff respond to my situation. This sort of thing happens all the time when an inmate asks me what I did to get here, because they say I obviously do not belong here. When I tell them I used to own an investment company and explain the situation, and I got thirty years for it, they are shocked and reply I should have killed someone or robbed them at gunpoint, which would have gotten me less time. The next words out of their mouths are always "That's ridiculous!" Then they want me to tell them how I did it. They want to do the same thing when they get out. LOL. Of course, I always decline to explain that to them.

Staff members are a little different when they ask because they usually already know why I am here and how long my sentence is. They look up all the inmates. They are different because they want to know all the stuff I owned and the lifestyle I lived. With regards to the length of my sentence, they all seem to ask the same question, "Who did you piss off?" It amazes me how many people come to the same conclusion—that thirty years is absurd—and agree it was all for publicity and political gain. They come to this conclusion without me ever suggesting it. They all say the same thing, "Child molesters, rapists, violent offenders, career offenders—all tend to get less time."

*****

Once I got the job at TCCI, I had to move to the school block. I went from a very quiet block where everyone worked long hours and were tired and quiet when they were not working, to a block with a bunch of juveniles with lots of pent-up energy and frustration.

At TCCI the blocks are arranged in color-coded units of three blocks each, with a separate lobby area called the D-Ring, because of its shape. Each unit was shaped like three prongs of a Star of David, with each block coming off the center D-Ring to a point. Each block had a dayroom in the middle flanked by two floors of cells and a shower area on each floor at the front next to the D-Ring. The dayroom had tables in the center with an open area at the front and rear. There were two televisions, a microwave, and some phones. The wall facing the D-Ring was all glass and was two stories tall.

The officers stayed in the D-Ring except to make rounds in the blocks about once or twice each hour. The education block was a zoo. It was like being in a big room with about a hundred two-year-olds running wild, yelling, and horsing around, fighting, singing and rapping out music on the doors. All in all, it was a very stressful experience. I pretty much stayed in my room except to watch something on TV or do Bible study with the Christian guys.

It was in this block that I saw my first real prison fight. Most prison fights are private matters and take place in the privacy of someone's room behind closed doors. That way, they avoid the involvement of officers and the potential of being sent to segregation—called "the hole"—for fighting. Occasionally, they happen in the dayroom, but I never saw one of those while at TCCI. My first witness of a fight happened one evening, not long after moving to the school block. I was sitting with some of my Christian friends watching TV when I heard a cell door shut to my left. I turned toward the noise to see through the door window two guys beating each other. I was so shocked. I had never actually seen a real fight in my life. I stood up and said to the guys with me that there were two guys fighting and we needed to do something and tell the officers. They quickly told me to shut up, sit down, and mind my own business. I did, but I kept looking over to watch. The fight only lasted a few minutes. The door opened, and the guy who did not live there left quickly to go to his room to change his torn, bloody shirt and clean up his bloody face while the other guy did the same. That was it. It was over that quick. Later on, the two guys were friends again. It beat all I had ever seen. I was a nervous wreck the rest of the night, but it was not a big deal to everyone else. I have seen many fights since, and I will never get used to it like these guys. Many times, the guys do not remain friends; many times, they do. I still do not get it, but then, I did not grow up like these guys. Fights are an everyday thing for them on the street. It is how most things are settled.

I had my first contact visit at TCCI. I was so nervous. It had been sixteen months since I had any physical contact with my family. It was a very happy and emotional two hours for us. They had driven over three and one-half hours to come see me. They continued to come every week. Visits are great. I looked forward to them each week, but I did not look forward to the end of the two hours when they had to leave. I never watched them leave; it is simply too depressing.

Most inmates never get visits or, at best, have visits once or twice a year. One of the biggest reasons they do not get them is that their family members and friends cannot get approved to enter the prison. The others are because of a lack of transportation or money. To be honest, most inmates would rather their families send them money than come to visit. I thank God for the blessing of a family whom I could not keep away if I tried. I could not make it through each day without their love and support.

I had been at TCCI about a month and a half when I went to the visitation area expecting to see Gilda, the kids, and my parents. When I walked in, Gilda and Hannah were not there. Mom and Dad were waiting along with Judge. I was confused and immediately worried. I knew something was not right. My thoughts initially went to Gracie, my mother-in-law, and I felt afraid something had happened to her. I was wrong in thinking Gracie, but right that something had happened. Gilda's sister, Teresa, had suddenly died that morning. I was numb and in shock.

My best friend, Ace, had died from cancer while I was at CCDC, but Teresa was the first immediate family member to die since my arrest. Since November 7, 2008, numerous friends and family have died. Prison causes things such as deaths, birthdays, anniversaries, holidays, and major news events to affect you differently. The physical disconnect with the "real world" on the outside causes everything happening there to seem surreal. They still affect you. You still shed tears and may experience some sadness and grief, or happiness, but there is not the deep personal connection to the event. Maybe it is the body or perhaps the soul's way of protecting us, but the longer I am locked up, the less and less I feel things, and the tougher aspects of my hide become more apparent.

Maybe it is the whole male, macho thing. You never really have true 100 percent privacy in prison to feel, cry, wail, or scream. I have a "private" single cell, and it still never feels like I can be alone. I guess you just begin to wall yourself off from everything, because if you do not, you will go completely crazy. On a positive note, I have learned to immediately and completely surrender every situation to the Lord.

The greatest test of this surrender came in November 2017 when Gilda found out she had leukemia. What a punch to the stomach. She had one of the acute forms of the cancer. In one day, she went from being a productive self-supporting citizen and caregiver to being unemployable, disabled, and in need of care herself. She spent the next six weeks in the hospital for her first round of treatments. The next round was an experimental treatment at home to be followed up by a bone marrow transplant. Over the next year, she spent many nights in the hospital battling infections and recurrences of the cancer. She and I talked on the phone often during all this, and we agreed she was in a win-win situation. If God healed her, she won; if He took her home, she won. We both were at peace, trusting His sovereignty in our lives. Finally on October 18, 2018, the Lord called Gilda home.

As prepared as I thought I was, I was not. Although we have not been able to be physically together on a daily basis we have been "one with God" as husband and wife for over thirty-three years. If you take into account the many years we dated, we have been together for nearly forty years. I am at total peace with the Lord's sovereignty in losing Gilda. I have a new understanding of Job's words following the death of his children and the loss of all his possessions in Job 1:21, "The LORD gave, and the LORD has taken away; blessed be the name of the LORD." I have experienced that "peace of the LORD" that passes all understanding, but I was not prepared for the void left by her absence. I am thankful for the life God gave us, and I am thankful that Gilda is now in His presence. I am even envious of her right now.

The day she died was the first day of a Kairos weekend at Mountain View Correctional Institute (MVCI). God provided many brothers in Christ who surrounded me and held me up and lifted me up before the throne of God. They embraced me as I cried or gave me the space and time alone to weep and grieve. My best friend at the time was Robert Deese. He sat with me while I grieved. Inmates do not hug in prison, but Robert hugged me when I needed it and let me cry on his shoulder.

The Lord planned her passing beautifully to provide the comfort and love I needed. The administration at MVCI was very supportive and kind through my grieving. In medium-custody prison in North Carolina, you are only allowed to attend a viewing with two people who are on your visitation list. Gilda was cremated, so there was no viewing.

I have said before, things affect you differently in prison. There is surrealism to major life events like losing a spouse. I have days when I handle it very well, then I have days when I feel many things, even anger at Gilda for dying and guilt for feeling that way. Many days, it just does not seem possible that she is gone for the rest of my life.

Judge, our youngest son, got married in December 2018 without either parent being present. Hannah, our youngest daughter, got married in 2019 without either parent being present. That is very hard for me. She is my baby girl. I want to be there for her. I wanted to be there to fulfill my God-given responsibility for all my children as their earthly father.

The only way to deal with this without going completely crazy is to surrender all to the Lord. However, most inmates go completely crazy rather than seek the peace of the Lord that comes with surrender. I realized this in one of my many people watching times, when I just sit and observe people. I have always been an avid people watcher and analyzer. I observed that inmates appear to be frozen in time, based on when they came to prison. Their mannerisms, their hairstyle, their vocabulary all reflect the era in which they lived on the street. I believe this is one of the major factors in their social failure when released. I see men all the time who were incarcerated when they were thirteen or fourteen and who have been raised by the system for maybe five or ten years. When released, they usually come back to prison within a year. They continue to find and stay in trouble. They often had the maturity level of a five-year-old at the age of thirteen or fourteen and never matured much beyond that. Now they are in their late thirties to midforties, stuck in a never-ending state of being a child in an adult body. I am reminded of the scripture in 1 Corinthians 13:11, "When I was a child, I spoke like a child, I thought like a child, I reasoned like a child. When I became a man, I gave up childish ways." These inmates have never grown beyond their childish words, thoughts, reasoning—all their childish ways. They have never had the benefit of having anyone mentor them into being a mature man.

*****

Visits are "antiseptic" visits. You can hug your family upon entering and when the visit is over, but there is no physical contact during the visit. The inmate sits in a chair facing the visitors, with about a four-foot distance between. If there are children young enough to sit in your lap, you are permitted to hold them. Still, it is a great time just being with your family in the same room.

One day, at TCCI, I was at work and was called to go to visitation. I went down the long hall to the slider doors at visitation. The female officer working in the control booth asked me where I was going. I was like, "You called me. I have a visit." She told me to show her my pass. I asked her, "What pass? You called me from work. I don't have a pass." She told me to go back to the unit and get a visitation pass.

I just smiled, like I am always doing, and I went all the way back to the officer in the D-Ring on Blue Unit, which was not a short trip, and got a pass. I was practically laughing the whole way because I knew what she was doing. She was trying to get a reaction out of me. She was hoping I would get angry and go off on her. I did not. I was grinning when I got back to the slider doors and held up the pass for her to see. Before she would open the door, she asked, "What are you grinning about?"

I almost burst out laughing. I responded, "I am happy because I have a visit."

That is the kind of people who worked at TCCI, and why I could not wait to get transferred. I had to wait six months. As soon as the six months were up, I did the paperwork to get away from TCCI and closer to home.

*****

I had already completed some research on other prisons closer to home prior to leaving CCDC. There are two medium-custody prisons within thirty minutes of home, but both are very rough facilities. Within an hour and a half, there are a few more. Of those, there was only one that fit the criteria I was looking for: single or double cells, no open dorms, air conditioning, and predominantly white. Not that I am racist—some of my best friends are black or Hispanic—but facilities where the majority of inmates are ethnic minority groups tend to be much rougher and unsafe places to spend thirty years. I was looking long term. I settled on Mountain View Correctional Institution (MVCI) in Spruce Pine. It is about an hour and a half from home.

I put in my transfer paperwork and was approved. Now I just had to wait for my name to move up to the top of the waiting list for MVCI. Surprisingly, that only took about two months, and I was back on the bus trip from hell for another fourteen-hour ride. Fortunately, this time the bus was only half-full for half the trip. From the transfer point at Sandy Ridge, the bus was only about half-full and would be making stops at four facilities before ending up at MVCI. It was about 7:00 p.m. when we arrived, and since there were only two of us left on the bus, processing was pretty easy. So far so good.

Then as I was walking down the main hallway trying to decide if I was going the right way, I met a man who did not have teeth, had strange eyes, and was bald except for sprigs of hair mostly on the back of his head and down his neck. He had a gimpy gait and wore glasses. He reminded me of a character from the movie *The Hills Have Eyes* or *Wrong Turn*. I asked him for directions and could barely understand his response. I immediately thought, *What have I gotten myself into?* I later got to know the man, and the saying is true, you cannot judge a book by its cover.

Like every facility, you have a mixture of staff that is very good, and some you want to avoid at all cost. It has been my experience, from the start at MVCI. A majority of the staff are good people who treat the inmates like fellow human beings. As with any new experience in our lives—new community, new school, new job, new church, new relationships—we have to get to know people, and we have to prove ourselves. I have been at MVCI since October 2010, and I have proven myself to be trustworthy, a good worker, not a troublemaker, someone set apart by my beliefs and my integrity, and definitely not your typical inmate.

I stand out to both inmates and staff because, as they will all tell you, I do not belong here. I hope I never cross over that line where I blend in with the crowd. I am not saying I am better than anyone here, but I am better educated, better behaved, and more mature.

I have to work very hard to maintain my sanity. It takes lots of prayer and Bible study. It is all too easy to become numb to your surroundings, to life beyond the fence. It is all too easy to lose your individuality, your personality, and become institutionalized. You go through the day-to-day routines of a set schedule, set meals, being told when and what to do, with very few real personal choices to make on your own. You begin to lose your awareness of your sur-roundings. Then it all comes crashing back to your consciousness. The walls, the people, the noises, the *everything* of this hell hits you in the face; and you just want to die.

A prison can be many things. I think I have a very real under-standing of what people feel like who are shut-ins in their homes, in nursing homes, in hospitals, in paralyzed bodies that no longer function; and it is not good. There are many similarities between their lives and prison. I am sure they feel as though they are in prison. Only through the comfort and help of the Holy Spirit in me, and the love of God through my family and brothers and sisters in Christ, can I maintain any semblance of sanity and can say I am full of joy. I say thank-you! I thank all of you who reach out to me with some godly love in many big and small ways. I have to constantly look forward to the day when all this will be behind me. I think of Christ and for the joy set before Him He endured the cross. My temporary suffering is nothing compared to what He went through to carry my sins on the cross. My life is great because of Him, and I have hope and a future.

Although MVCI is far from the ideal prison situation, it is also far from the situation at TCCI. They are polar opposites. I have been here long enough that the staff recognizes my family and vice versa. I am not saying we are all buddy-buddy, but it is nice when an officer notices the growth and maturity of your children, or notices that someone has not been to visit in a while and asks about their welfare. They respect me and my family, and we respect them. They know they can trust us. They do not have to be concerned about my visitors trying to smuggle anything in to me because that is not who I am or who we are as a family. I have seen many instances of a parent, grandparent, child, or relative getting caught smuggling drugs to their loved one.

*****

If you only listen to the media and the Barrys and Glendas, you may have a distorted view of who I am. You may be able to garner a very one-sided list of some of my deeds, my sins, but these are not a true picture of who I am. Those things are—or rather, were—a part of me the person, but not me the child of God. The true me cannot be ascertained by looking at a few deeds and sins in my life.

Let me show you what I mean with a biblical example. By all indications from Scripture, David had a strong and unique relationship with God early on in his life. As a young shepherd boy, the runt of the litter in his father's house, God knew David's potential, and most importantly, God knew David's heart. We know this because God tells us so in 1 Samuel 16:7, "For the Lord sees not as man sees; man looks on the outward appearance, but the Lord looks on the heart."

I am so thankful that God knows my heart, the true me. What frustrates me is how quickly we forget what we know about a person's heart when their sins are brought into the light of media scrutiny. It is part of our human nature in a fallen world. We do not have to look further than the daily newscasts or newspapers to confirm it. I do not know an exact figure, but I am willing to bet the percentage of news reported daily that is good news as opposed to pain, suffering, disaster, or scandal is probably 1 percent or less.

I am reminded of a 1982 Don Henley song, "Dirty Laundry."

> The bubble-headed bleached blonde…
> [tells us] 'bout the plane crash with a gleam in her eye…
> Dirty little secrets, dirty little lies
> We got our dirty little fingers in everybody's pie…
> We all know that crap is king
> Give us dirty laundry!

Wow! What an accurate assessment of our obsession with other people's sins and troubles.

I am sure many of you know the story of the invention of dynamite, but it is worthy of mentioning again. The man who invented dynamite did so with good in mind and with the intention of creating bigger and better weapons. Dynamite was to be a safer way to blow things up. He became disheartened over his reputation as a man of war, death, and destruction. He could not bear the thought of dying and being known as the inventor of dynamite. He decided to do something to leave a legacy of peace so people would remember who he truly was and maybe forget his invention. His name was Alfred Nobel, and he created a foundation from his dynamite fortune to promote peace in the world. The foundation would award prizes to people who did extraordinary things to promote peace. He succeeded. Today he is remembered for the Nobel Peace prize and who he really was in his heart, and only marginally as the inventor of dynamite.

A more modern example would be Charles "Chuck" Colson. Mr. Colson was President Nixon's henchman in the Watergate scandal that cost him the presidency. Mr. Colson went to prison, was saved by the grace of God, and founded Prison Fellowship, the world's largest prison ministry. Few people remember his criminal past, but nearly everyone has heard of Prison Fellowship and his legacy of who he really was lives on today in the ministry.

Let us go back to the biblical example of David. According to Scripture, he was not a great parent, not a great husband; he was a man who committed adultery and murder. He made mistakes as a king, which cost seventy thousand Israelite lives. However, despite all his shortcomings, he is the only man God calls "a man after My own heart." What made David that endearing to God? I believe it was his integrity. How could he do all those things, commit the sins of adultery and murder, cause seventy thousand to lose their lives because of his disobedience, and still have integrity? To which I would ask you, how could he not have integrity and be a man after God's own heart?

What is integrity? *Webster's New College Dictionary* says it is "a firm adherence to a code or standard of values; probity—a complete uprightness; the state of being unimpaired—soundness; the quality or condition of being undivided—completeness." You say that does not sound like David at all. No, it does not. If you only see David as man sees him, from the outside, I agree. However, we are not the ones making the judgment about David's intentions, his integrity— God is. God says in 1 Samuel 16:7, "For the Lord sees not as man sees; man looks on the outward appearance, but the Lord looks on the heart."

When God looks on David, He does not see his failures as a parent, husband, or king; nor does He see David's sins. Why? Because David's sins have been removed as far as the east is from the west. He sees David through the cross of Christ, the blood of Christ that has atoned for his sins, washing him whiter than snow and making him a new creation. We want to look at David's failures and sins because "we all know that crap is king. Give us dirty laundry!" If we dare to look at David as God does, with all that crap stripped away, what do we have left? I believe it is his integrity.

Let us look at Scripture and see if we can see what God sees. In 1 Samuel 16 the prophet Samuel anoints David, a young adolescent shepherd runt, as the next king of Israel; and the Holy Spirit rushed upon David from that day forward. I take this to mean David was filled with the Holy Spirit. There must have been a time lapse between the anointing in verse 13 to David going to serve King Saul in verse 18. This time was significant in David's life. He was growing and maturing in his walk with the Lord under the teaching of the Holy Spirit. In verse 18, King Saul's servant calls David a man skilled in playing the lyre, a man of valor and war, prudent in speech, good-looking, and lastly, but most importantly, a man of God. However long this time lapse was, David's reputation preceded him all the way to the king's house in Jerusalem. Does not that sound like a man of integrity? "Yes," you say, "but he has not fallen into his grievous sins yet." I agree.

The next event in David's life is his battle with Goliath in chapter 17. He is still a young man, but look at the wisdom, the depth of relationship and understanding he has with God, and the bravery, confidence, and assurance of success he has as well. The Israelites have been cowering in fear from Goliath for a while now with no hope of a win. David comes in and states what should have been obvious to Saul and his army. "Who is this uncircumcised Philistine that he should defy the armies of the living God?" Saul hears of it, the sound of first real hope he has had, and calls David in. David says, "Let no man's heart fail because of him [Goliath]. Your servant will go fight with this Philistine." Saul tries to dress him up for battle in the king's armor and sword, but they do not fit. They are made for a grown man, and David is not quite there yet. He says, "The Lord who delivered me from the paw of the lion and from the paw of the bear will deliver me from the hand of this Philistine."

Are you listening to what David is saying? These three times, his focus is on the Lord. This battle is not about him or the Israelite army or the king; it is about believing and trusting in the Lord. It is the Lord's battle, and victory is assured.

Neither is David a fool. He picks up five smooth stones to take into battle, his ammunition. He understood that when we go into battle, we should always fight as if it is all about the Lord but prepare as if it is all about us. He is not cocky and only takes one stone. He is humble and takes five stones.

I do not know why five, but I am guessing that in his experience with the lion and the bear, maybe he has already calculated the distance to Goliath and determined he would only have five chances to throw a stone before reaching the giant. (Some believe the other four were for Goliath's brothers.) Therefore, he was not overconfident and only took one. This is a sign of integrity. I still hear you agreeing, but with the disclaimer that he has not fallen yet.

The first major sin in David's life comes in 2 Samuel 11—Bathsheba. Well, the sin really was not Bathsheba herself. It was lust and coveting his neighbor's wife, which led to adultery, which led to murder, which led to the death of his son.

I can hear you. "A-ha! This is the beginning of his downfall. This is when he first lost his integrity." I disagree in that I do not think David ever lost his integrity. What? How could I say that? Is this not the beginning of people losing their faith in their king? Losing their trust? I agree, yes, but none of that has anything to do with his integrity—at least, not his *true* integrity: his integrity with God.

What other kind of integrity is there? None. None that is worth anything. Did some lose faith in their king? Yes. Did some lose trust? Yes. However, what we are talking about is the *whole* of David, not the individual sins he committed. True integrity is not what others think of you or the amount of faith or trust they have in you. It is about how God sees you.

Remember *Webster's* definition: "a firm adherence to a code or standard of values; probity—complete uprightness; the state of being unimpaired—soundness; the quality or condition of being undivided—completeness."

Still does not sound like David? God knew all of David's life from beginning to end, before Samuel ever recorded God calling David a man after His own heart in 1 Samuel 13:15.

Can we see in Scripture evidence of the true David? I think we can. I believe his sins were eating his heart out. I think he wanted desperately to confess and be forgiven, but he was afraid—afraid of how others would think and react. He knew the circumstances of Saul's losing the throne; he knew God to be a fair, just, wrathful, and merciful God. He was paranoid and afraid and, I think, lonely. He physically, emotionally, and spiritually felt separated from God. The Holy Spirit, which had rushed upon him years earlier and remained with him, was grieving inside him over his sins. All he needed was a push, and God was about to give it to him.

Look at 2 Samuel 12. This is the account of the prophet Nathan confronting David with his sins. His sins were grievous before the Lord. Nathan said he, David, "utterly scorned the Lord." God announced, through Nathan, David's punishment and the consequences of his sins, which are severe but not life-threatening—at least, not to David's life. In the midst of these punishments, Nathan also said a very important thing from God to David. He said in verse 13, "The Lord also has put away your sins." Just before that, in the same verse, David confessed, "I have sinned against you, Lord." In God's eyes, David is not defined by these sins; they have been put aside. David is defined by his heart.

Look at 2 Samuel 12:15–23. Following Nathan's rebuke, the child born to David and Bathsheba became sick. For some days, David fasted and poured out his heart to God on behalf of the child. The elders and servants were worried because David would not eat. He was distraught. They were by his side continuously. By the way, does that sound like a person who has lost his integrity? I think not. They are scared to tell him the child has died, fearing he may take his own life.

See David's response to the child's death in verses 20–23? He arose from sitting in the dirt, cleaned up, put on clean clothes, and went to worship the Lord. Afterward, he went home and ate. All those around him were dismayed about his response. He did not get more upset, he did not hurt himself, and he did not curse God. He straightened himself up and worshipped the holy, sovereign God. David understood God so profoundly and deeply, in a way only a man of *true* integrity could. No, I say, David never lost his integrity, even in periods of great sin in his life.

Now why have I spent so much time on David and his integrity? How have I concluded what David felt? What could I know about the depth of his understanding and relationship with God? I have always loved David, even from childhood. There are so many life lessons to be learned from him. I have grown up learning from David. Still, it was not until my life slowed down long enough—fifteen months, to be exact—that I allowed the Holy Spirit to teach me the really deep truths from David's life. In the depths of my depression while at CCDC, God comforted me and lifted me up from that pit with the truth of integrity in David's life.

When Cris would visit me on Fridays at CCDC, we would discuss what I was studying in God's Word. He would ask from where this depth of truth was coming. What was it all about?

I have always felt connected somehow personally with David, a kindred spirit. I do not mean anything mystical, but like brothers in Christ. The way you instantly have a bond with some complete stranger, and you find out they are a believer. When you have been deeply forgiven, and you meet someone who has also experienced that kind of forgiveness and love, there is a real and unique understanding of one another.

Knowing the Lord intimately has always been a part of who I am. There is not a day that goes by where I do not ponder that relationship and thank God for choosing to save me. I know it seems so contradictory, my saying that in comparison to the sin in my life. I cannot explain it. If you are not a believer—or even if you are a believer but have not let God touch you with His deepest love and forgiveness—then you will never understand it. However, if you have, then you know what I am talking about. God says through the prophet Isaiah in the book by his name, chapter 55, verses 8 and 9, "For my thoughts are not your thoughts, neither are your ways my ways, declares the LORD. For as the heavens are higher than the earth, so are my ways higher than your ways and my thoughts than your thoughts." There are just some things, some truths, we cannot explain. That is why we have faith. "Now faith is the assurance of things hoped for, the conviction of things not seen" (Hebrews 11:1).

How then have I concluded David's feelings? I believe I have been where David has been. I have not committed adultery or murder. My grievous sins are much different than his, but it matters not what the sins are; it is all about the relationship, the heart.

I said earlier I believe his sins were eating his heart out. That is not an exclusive feeling of David's. It is a universal truth for all true believers. I said I believe he was desperate to confess. Again, not an exclusive feeling of David's but another universal truth for all believers. I think those are evident in Scripture when Nathan confronts David in 2 Samuel 12:7 and says, "You are the man!" David immediately confesses. He does not try to get out of it. He could have. After all, he was king. What he says goes. No, he was tired of the lies, the guilt, and the brokenness of his relationship with his Lord.

Yes, I have been where David has been. Perhaps you have too. Perhaps you are there right now. Please, I beg you; do not stay in the darkness. Confess. Bring whatever it is, into the light. Trust me, all the punishment, all the consequences will be worth it for the peace and restored relationship with the Lord.

November 7, 2008, was my day of reckoning, but I still could not do it on my own. I needed my own Nathan to knock on my door with a gun on his side and a jacket that said, "NC Secretary of State" plastered on the back to say, "You are the man!" That presence gave me the wakeup call I needed, the push to pray for God to do whatever had to be done to end it all and bring Himself glory for it.

Like David, I was still "king" that day when the agents showed up with a search warrant. That is all they had. I was not under arrest. Even though I could not stop them from doing their job and taking anything they wanted, I was nonetheless free to leave. I could have chosen to keep my mouth shut. I could have left the house, gone to the bank and cleaned out the accounts, and begun liquidating assets. By the time they were done sifting through the truckload of stuff they took, weeks would have passed, and I could have been out of the country. I could have gone to a place with no extradition agreement with the United States. However, I could not do that, would not do that. No way would I leave my family, and no way would I take them with me. I would not leave all this mess for them to deal with. Leaving has been the only advice I have gotten from people when I tell them my story. "Oh, that's not what I would have done," they say. *They* referencing the inmates (go figure) and guards (go figure again). I am amazed that this is always people's solution. Everyone thought I would run except my family and those who truly know my heart.

These are people who see me the way God sees me, a man after His own heart too.

*****

I shake my head whenever I take a step back and try to analyze how and why my life came to the point of such epic and grandiose failure. By sharing this analysis, I hope to accomplish two goals: one, to help you better understand me; and two, to issue a warning for your own life. I have identified four specific areas: pride, peer pressure, love of money, and greed. These are only subheadings of the overall issue of the war between the flesh and the spirit. It all boils down to this war each of us is engaged in, on a cosmic scale. Although it is an epic battle, the strategy to fight is not that complex. Yet it is extremely hard for us to follow most of the time. To win this war, we have to do two things.

First, keep a steady focus on God and your goal for eternity. If your focus is 100 percent on God, your thinking will be clear, your whole being filled with His wisdom. You will clearly hear the voice of the Holy Spirit as He teaches and guides your spirit. We will not give in to the attacks of Satan and the desires of your own fallen flesh.

What is your goal for eternity? Did you know we each have one of two goals for eternity? Have you ever thought of eternity in terms of having a goal? You should. It helps keep the focus. Eternity is not the goal. We already have that waiting for each of us. There are only two eternities, one with God and one without God. My goal is eternity with God.

If the goal does not reach past tomorrow, we have already lost the war between the flesh and the spirit. If that is where you are at, you have already conceded defeat. This flesh we occupy here and now, this existence, this life we are living—the worldly part, at least—has no future in eternity. It ends here in the span of eighty to a hundred years. That is all.

"That is all?" you say.

Are you saying you think a hundred years seems like an eternity? Then your perspective is all wrong. A hundred years in the light of eternity is like one tiny grain of sand in all the grains of sand on the earth. That is an incalculable amount of grains of sand! A hundred years is nothing.

Second, walk in the spirit, not in the flesh. Focus is the biggest part of the battle and the most important, but not the most difficult. The hardest part is walking in the spirit. This is the part where you have to say no to the flesh. When we do this, the flesh rears its ugly head and starts whining and pitching temper tantrums. We are no different than the spoiled child whose parents always give in to the whining and tantrums. We have become a whole nation of whiny brats. "Gimme, gimme, gimmie" has become the mantra of the world. We are a people of entitlements. "Give me what I want! You owe it to me!" What? The only thing we are owed is eternity in hell, which we can have freely. This is living in the flesh.

The other, more valuable, thing we can have freely is salvation, which takes us out of a hell-bound life to a life of peace in the Lord. Salvation is free; eternity with God is free to us. It is a gift. There is nothing we can do to pay for it or earn it. However, it is the most costly gift ever given, because it cost God the life of His Son. It cost Christ His life to ransom ours.

The thing is, we cannot fully walk in the spirit and hold on to any part of the flesh at the same time, and it is equally impossible to separate ourselves from the flesh. We cannot look on Christ with our heart and look on our neighbor's wife or possessions with our eyes. When we start rationalizing our sins as little glances at Bathsheba bathing on the rooftop, we have already conceded defeat to the flesh. We have compromised. Pride, peer pressure, love of money, and greed were my areas of compromise.

Everything about the BFG was out of character for me. When I look back and ask myself how I could have done all of this wrong and hurt all these people, there is only one answer: sin.

Sin is how. More specifically, the sin of pride is how. All of us underestimate the power of sin, flesh, and Satan in our lives. I do not care who you are, or how strong of a walk you have or think you have with the Lord, there are times when you let your guard down, and sin woos you from walking in the light to walking in the dark. Maybe it is only for a moment, and you are able to recognize it for what it is and pull yourself back on path. Maybe you are there right now, in the midst of a downfall, and do not even know it is happening until it reaches a point of no return. Maybe you are there right now and do realize it, and you feel trapped and hopeless.

Please hear me when I tell you, DO NOT GIVE UP! There is hope. There is a way out. There is help, both spiritually and physically. You have to be willing to surrender everything to Christ and confess both to Him and to somebody. Without Christ and someone physically holding you accountable, there is no hope. However, with Christ and accountability, there is nothing in heaven or on earth that God cannot handle or that can separate you from His love and forgiveness. Trust me in this. I am not just someone with some knowledge, wisdom, or advice to impart. I am someone who has lived through the nightmare and experienced the freedom and joy that comes with surrendering all to Christ and confessing.

More importantly, trust in God's Word in Romans 8:31–39,

> If God is for us, who can be against us? He who did not spare His own Son gave Him up for us all, how will He not also with Him graciously give us all things? Who shall bring any charge against God's elect? It is God who justifies. Who is to condemn? Christ Jesus is the one who died—more than that, who was raised, who is at the right hand of God, who indeed is interceding for us. Who shall separate us from the love of Christ? Shall tribulation, or distress, or persecution, or famine, or nakedness, or danger, or sword? …in all these things we are more than conquerors through Him who loved us. For I am sure that neither death, nor life, nor angels, nor rulers, nor things present nor things to come, nor powers, nor height, nor depth, nor anything else in all creation, will be able to separate us from the love of God in Christ Jesus our Lord.

I saw a T-shirt once that said, "Come to the dark side… We've got cookies." Isn't that how it works? Our flesh loves the darkness (and cookies). Things are more fun and exciting in the dark, right? Would you enjoy or want to go to a haunted house at Halloween if it was all lit up and bright? Why are they never open during the daytime? Or would you be drawn into the scary scenes of a movie if the victims turned on the lights in every room of the house before going in? Why, in these movies, does all the bad stuff happen in darkness? Because that is where evil thrives, and that's where evil keeps the cookies we so desire. I mean, how bad can it be; they have the cookies, right?

The book of Proverbs is full of practical timeless wisdom. Chapters 7 and 9 specifically speak to the lure of darkness through the adulteress and the woman, "folly." They seduce the young man, "lacking sense," into their boudoir. He does not know that it leads to Sheol, the place of the dead, until it's too late. He is thinking with the flesh, not the spirit. He is thinking *Cookies*. That one little compromise is so often our downfall into slavery to sin, flesh, and Satan.

That is where I was for seventeen years. Every passing day, giving a new piece of myself over to the slavery and the lies of the evil trio—sin, flesh, Satan. I am here to tell you, whatever the evil trio is feeding you, you can count on only one thing: it is a lie. Oh, there may be a lot of truth thrown into the mix to make the poison palatable, but it is still deadly, and it is certainly not *the truth*.

The sin of pride goes all the way back before God created man to the fall of Satan. God speaks through the prophet Ezekiel, in the book by his name, chapter 28, verses 1–19, a lament over the king of Tyre, which is also a comparison of the king with Satan. God says,

> You were blameless in your ways from the
> day you were created, till unrighteousness was
> found in you… Your heart was proud because of
> your beauty; you corrupted your wisdom for the
> sake of your splendor.

Satan's pride was in his beauty, his appearance. From there his appearance became an idol, which led to compromises in other areas, all for the sake of the idol. Appearance or beauty does not have to be physical. It can be a reputation, a social status, a career, or anything that for you can become an idol—a slave master.

For me it was my reputation, my appearance to others, my pride. What others perceived of me became the bait and snare. Let's not forget Proverbs 16:18, "Pride goes before destruction, and a haughty spirit before a fall."

As Christians we have the power of Christ in us to overcome the evil trio, but we far too often do not use it. Why is that? Let's look at God's Word in 1 Peter 5:8, "Be sober-minded, be watchful. Your adversary the devil prowls around like a roaring lion, seeking someone to devour." Why does God use the simile, "prowls around like a roaring lion"? Why is Satan like a lion when he is "seeking someone to devour"? This is a very telling analogy. Lions love to hunt in the dark of night, in secret. Why? That is when the hunting is easiest and to their advantage. That is when the hunted is most vulnerable. They also hunt during the day if the opportunity presents itself, but they are at their best at night, in the dark.

God is not saying Satan only works under the cover of physical darkness. No, he is using darkness as a metaphor to things hidden, unacceptable, undiscerned, dirty, evil, wrong. We can be in the pit of absolute darkness, yet be standing physically in broad daylight.

Another point about lions is they are not big fluffy cats that you can play around with. No, they are deadly. They see everything as a meal to devour. They may look all lazy and cuddly lounging under the shade tree out on the savannah, yet they are anything but. Satan is like that, and sin is like that, and the flesh is like that, luring us in with all that beauty, pleasure, and wealth, until we are too close to escape in time. Then the devouring begins, a ravenous feeding frenzy.

God began this passage of Scripture in 1 Peter with, "Be sober-minded, be watchful." It is a command before a warning about Satan. We always have to be on guard, alert. When we are not, that is when we are most vulnerable to the attacks.

Have you ever been drunk physically from alcohol, or high from doing drugs? I can count on one hand the number of times in my life I have been drunk, and I have never been high on drugs. If you have been either drunk or high then you know from experience what I am about to say is true; if you have not, then you just have to trust me on this.

When you are drunk or high, you lose your inhibitions, and your conscience is incapacitated. The part of you that helps to reason, make good informed choices, and keep the desires of the flesh under control is compromised, and you do stupid things. You become extremely vulnerable to suggestions. Things, decisions that in a sober-minded, watchful state would never cross your mind will now appear to be perfectly logical things to do. The lion baring his large, sharp teeth at you from under the shade tree, which normally would scare you to death, all of a sudden seems to be a tame kitten beckoning you closer and closer to pet it.

Do not forget this is a command to be sober-minded and watchful. God says *be* these things. There is no option to choose or not. This is serious warfare. There is no room for compromise. If we are to be successful, we have to *be* both of these things—sober-minded and watchful.

God finished this passage in 1 Peter 5:9 with, "Resist him [Satan], firm in your faith, knowing that the same kinds of suffering are being experienced by your brotherhood throughout the world."

There are three things I want to talk about here.

First, "Resist him" (Satan). Again, this is a command. Notice God does not say, "Try to resist him," but "Resist him." I am 100 percent certain that you are guilty as am I of having said to God, "Lord, I'm trying to ________________." Fill in the blank with whatever it is you are making an excuse for *not* doing. I have come to hate the word *trying*, and I believe God does as well, when we use it to precede an excuse for not doing what He commands us to do. He does not give us things to do if He is not first going to equip us to do them. If He has equipped us, then we cannot help but be successful.

God says again in James 4:7, "Resist the devil, and he will flee from you." It is the same command, only this time, God adds a promise. Notice what God does *not* say. He does *not* say Satan *might* flee or *sometimes* flees. No, He says Satan *will* flee. This is a very powerful promise. There is comfort and confidence in this promise. Do not be misled. If it were not so, God would not have said it. He would not have told James to write it down for us.

The second thing God tells us in the 1 Peter passage is *how* to resist Satan. He says, "Resist him, firm in the faith." I like how the Amplified Bible expands the word *firm*. It says, "rooted, established, strong, immovable, and determined." Who does not like being told clearly and specifically how to do something? All the guesswork is removed. You have the assurance of success from an expert in this passage, who has "been there, done that." Christ, Emmanuel, God with us, had to resist Satan when He was in the wilderness of temptation.

Although Jesus was physically weak from going without food for forty days, He was still sober-minded and watchful. Being sober-minded and watchful has nothing to do with our physical state of being and neither does our firmness of faith. You can find this account recorded in Matthew 4:1–11. Jesus is our literal perfect example of being rooted, established, strong, immovable, and determined in everything. He resists Satan, firm in Himself, in who He is. He is God incarnate. As flesh and blood like us, He was vulnerable to all the same fleshly things we are.

He resists Satan firmly in God's Word. Remember when I said Satan would use enough truth to make the poison palatable? Well, this story is an example of just that. He misuses the truth of God's Word to try and trick Jesus, but Jesus is firm in the correct use of God's truth.

I believe Jesus also resists *firmly* in knowing the truth of the promise in James 4:7, if we resist Satan he will flee, which is exactly what happens in Matthew 4:11. However, notice that Satan does not immediately flee at the first resistance. James does not say how much resistance it takes to get him to flee. It is not just a one-time thing. Satan does not give up that easily. It may sometimes work that way, but not always—and in my experience, rarely.

What it does take is *complete* resistance. Firm, rooted, established, strong, immovable, and determined resistance. When Satan saw Jesus would not budge, then he fled. Christ's resistance was complete.

Finally, Jesus resists Satan by remaining firm in the truth. There is a bigger picture to consider. Satan tries to tempt Jesus with wealth and power. He appeals to the flesh for help bringing down the Son of God. Jesus resists *firmly* in the faith He already knows the end of Satan, and He knows His own reign as sovereign Lord and owner of all creation.

We also know the bigger picture. God's Word is clear about our future with Him at the end of time when Christ returns. We can stand firm in our faith on that truth. Hebrews 11 is filled with many examples of people who were firm in their faith. Yet these are not perfect examples. These people—Abraham, Sarah, Noah, Gideon, Samson, David and others—were at times not firm in their faith. At those times, they were colossal failures. It is that very fact of human-ness that encourages us to keep going. Humanity has not changed, and God has not changed either. We still serve the same God who blesses that same firmness in faith for us as He did for them.

When we are failing because of a lack of faith, we should not give up but confess our failure and return to what we know to be truth in our lives. We should return to the firmness that Christ, through the Holy Spirit, provides us.

I also love the definition of *faith* in Hebrews 11:1, "Now faith is the assurance of things hoped for, the conviction of things not seen." Wow! What an awesome, comforting, deep, and powerful definition.

The third thing I want to talk about from the 1 Peter 5 passage is the fact stating that we are not in this alone. God says, "Knowing that the same kinds of suffering are being experienced by your broth-erhood throughout the world." One of the greatest military strategies throughout history has been to divide and conquer. Satan under-stands and uses this better than anyone else.

There is strength in numbers and weakness in going solo. When we attempt to go it alone, we isolate ourselves from the benefit of the experience, wisdom, and accountability of others.

Satan tries to convince us we are the most heinous human being ever because of the things we have done, and that no one could ever understand us, love us, or forgive us if the truth ever came out. He will try to convince us there is no hope; we are very alone in our sin; no one could possibly understand what we are experiencing. He does not want us to confess. It is true others may not fully understand, because they have not had the exact same experiences or committed the exact same sin, but we have all experienced the effect of sin in our lives. Therefore, we can fully understand from the perspective of a sinner in need of forgiveness.

What happens when light shines into darkness? The darkness flees, right? It is no more. Darkness cannot exist where the light of truth exists. When we confess and seek the accountability of God and of our fellow Christians, it is the same as turning on a light in a dark room. When we realize the truth, that we are not alone, we can draw strength from our brotherhood throughout the world to resist *firmly* in the faith.

David was too proud to admit to Bathsheba's husband Uriah that he had slept with his wife. David could have gone to Uriah, confessed the sin, and took his chances with how he would have reacted. I am sure Uriah would have been angry, but over time, he may have come to forgive the king. What could he have done? David was king. David could have anything he wanted, and who could have denied him?

Pride goes hand in hand with peer pressure. Some would say they are one and the same. I think not. Pride is more personal. Peer pressure is more public. It would be quicker to say *peer pressure* is more synonymous with *paranoia*. I think peer pressure can be more powerful than pride. We always put more emphasis on what other people think than what God thinks, and we give other people way too much credit and power over us.

David learned, once confronted with his sins, that the people still loved him, still wanted him as king, and forgave him. His fear of peer pressure was totally unfounded. If they were willing to forgive him for adultery and murder, surely they would have forgiven him for just adultery if he had confessed at the beginning. Nathan told him, after he confessed, that God had put away his sin; so obviously,

God would have done the same at the beginning, before the sin of lust turned into adultery, which turned into murder.

Pride was the beginning of my downfall. I was too proud to seek help when I had financial trouble at the beginning of BFG. I had all good intentions of running a successful business helping people reach their financial goals. However, I let pride get in the way. I know now, as I knew then, I could have confessed my problems to any number of people, and they would have helped me, but I was too prideful to ask.

Once my focus had shifted ever so slightly off trusting God with guiding me through this problem, the peer pressure kicked into high gear. It grew over the years to be the biggest of the four beasts in my life, because it became an overwhelming paranoia of everything.

I look back now and see so clearly how unfounded all that was. If I had only humbled myself—first before God, then before those few people involved in the beginning—I am certain there would have been forgiveness and help to right the wrong. However, I chose to believe the lie that I could turn this around; I could cover it all up, and eventually, it would work out or go away. Then you wake up, and not only have you committed adultery, but there is a baby involved, then a murder. Where does it stop? I know that is how David must have felt. That is how I felt. I woke up, and it seemed like all of a sudden there were hundreds of people involved, millions of dollars, seventeen years gone by, and an enormous, unsustainable cover-up. I just wanted out, but I did not know how to do that. I needed my personal Nathan to say, "You are the man!"

Thank you, God, for the Nathans in our lives. If you do not have a Nathan but need a Nathan, why not try asking God to send you one?

I believe in the truth of 1 Timothy 6:10, "For the love of money is a root of all kinds of evils." All through the history of man, money has been the object of idolatry for everyone. Yes, everyone. You may say, "I don't really love money, just what it can buy." It is the same thing. I do not believe all love of money is a sin. It is the type of love, or the reasons and or motivations behind the love. In the English language, we have the one word *love*. In the Bible, there are three words:

eros, phileo, and *agape*. To make my point about whether the love of money is a sin or not, I am going to use two of these words—*eros* and *phileo*. *Eros* is the passionate sexual kind of love. It is where we get our word *erotic*. *Phileo* is the brotherly kind of love. It is why the city of Philadelphia is called the City of Brotherly Love. When we *eros* money, it is a sin. When we *phileo* money, it is most likely not a sin.

What is the difference?

Eros is the most intimate form of love, the deepest commitment to a relationship. It is associated by the coming together of two into one. *Eros* is a covenant, a blood covenant. A covenant is like a contract, a legal agreement binding two parties to a mutually agreed-upon relationship. God speaks all through the Bible about His covenants with humanity. The highest, permanent form of covenant is a blood covenant. The covenant of salvation in Christ is a blood covenant involving the shedding of Christ's blood. This covenant is why we get so excited and passionate and humbled when we talk about being washed by the blood, covered by the blood, sealed by the blood, saved by the blood of Christ. It is a forever unbreakable covenant.

In society today, we have lost the importance of the biblical meaning of a blood covenant. Marriage is a blood covenant. Marriage has always been a blood covenant to God. How is it a blood covenant? It is a blood covenant through the act of sexual intercourse consummating the marriage relationship. When a virgin woman has sexual intercourse for the first time, the hymen membrane is broken, and there is a shedding of blood. The blood washes over the man, and in God's eyes creates the *eros* bond of marriage between the two, the blood covenant. That is why one of the legal grounds for annulling a marriage is if it has not been consummated, meaning there has not been sexual intercourse (the two becoming one flesh).

We have trampled on God's designs, trampled on the purpose and meaning of marriage today. We do not even recognize the fact it is intended to be a permanent, "until death do us part" relationship.

Eros love, in a biblical context, is a wonderful thing. However, when we give ourselves over to *eros* money, that is a sin. When we become one with money, almost in a sexual way, it is a sin. It begins to replace all other relationships around us. It becomes lust and idolatry. The second half of 1 Timothy 6:10 says, "It is through this craving that some have wandered away from the faith and pierced themselves with many pangs." That is what lust, idolatry—sin—does to us. Or rather we do to ourselves when we embrace sin.

No one, absolutely no one, is immune. No matter how much or how little money you have; this is a nondiscriminating, universal sin. It is a consuming passion. That is why I label it *eros*. Our sexual *eros*, the physical sex drive, is probably the strongest and hardest human trait to resist. The love of money is that strong. God says, through the good doctor Luke's Gospel, chapter 16, verse 13, "No servant can serve two masters, for either he will hate the one and love the other, or he will be devoted to the one and despise the other. You cannot serve God and money." What it really comes down to is, the love of money is the same as idolatry.

When we have a *phileo* type of love for money, a brotherly type of love, it is not necessarily a sin, unless it aligns with what Luke 16:13 is teaching. We can have a healthy relationship with money. When we see it as a tool for doing God's will and as a necessary tool for daily living in the world, it is not an idolatrous relationship. We are not serving money, but it is serving us—or rather, serving God.

The only way we can maintain this type of relationship with money is by winning the battle between the flesh and the spirit as outlined before. Once you have crossed that line, it seems impossible to ever go back. This is the power we give sin in our lives rather than living out of the power of Jesus Christ in our lives. After all, He tells us, "In the world you will have tribulation. But take heart; I have overcome the world" (John 16:33). We forget quickly that we have the power of the One Who created everything at our disposal to overcome anything the world throws at us.

I allowed the paranoia of having to be successful on an ever-increasing scale to lure me into a much stronger temptation to fall in *eros* with money. I already had a healthy *phileo* relationship with it. I had that all my life because of my upbringing. However, as the number of clients increased and the amount of money coming in increased, the lifestyle and pretense increased. First came the Porsche

Boxster, then an upgrade to a Porsche Carrera, then a Bluebird motor home, then the upgrade to a Prevost Vantare motor home, then a newer one with slide-outs, then the Mercedes S65 sedan, then the Aston Martin DB9, and thrown in along the way were two beach houses, a condo in the mountains, a boat, then a newer boat, two jet skis, various other vehicles, a myriad of construction equipment, quadrupling the size of our home, a new office, and on, and on, and on.

After you have had the taste of the good life and living the dream, you find you really like it. You stop staying in Motel 6 and start being a regular at the Ocean Club in the Bahamas. You start flying first class and stop getting cabins with windows on cruise ships and start booking suites with balconies on the concierge deck. You stop staying at the value-priced Disney hotels, and you own two thousand Disney Vacation Club points. You do not just have an American Express card; you have the black AMEX Centurion card made of metal instead of plastic.

Most of that was for the pretense of success, but to be perfectly honest, I loved it and hated it all at the same time. I was torn within as the battle between the flesh and the spirit raged. The flesh was obviously winning, but thank God, He never gave up on me. He kept the pressure up until I broke. That was until I had had all I could take and was willing to surrender all to Him. It was so easy at that point. Again, I beg you, if you are in the midst of that battle in your life, just give up. Surrender it all now. Let God have control. You will not believe the peace awaiting you.

Greed is next. Greed is different from the love of money; although, still very nearly the same. Love of money is about a relationship, about idolatry. Greed is about an insatiable want of more. It is about being selfish. They seem to be one and the same; however, there is a profound difference.

Many would say my lifestyle and all the possessions listed above and the constant upgrades sure look and sound like greed to them. I know it looks that way, but it is not. It definitely could be greed, but for me it was not and comes down to me, my character, and my spiritual gifts.

Because we are ambitious creatures, we will always want more of everything. Ambition itself is not a sin if kept under control, and we keep it under control by learning and practicing the admonition in Hebrews 13:5. This text says to be content with what we have. Paul's teaching in Philippians 4:11 is similar: "For I have learned in whatever situation I am to be content."

Contentment is one of the hardest states of being—if not the hardest—to achieve in society today. Everywhere we turn we see, hear, smell, taste, and touch things that attack our contentment. Every ad we see or hear, every loaf of fresh-baked bread or warm fudge we smell, every hot Krispy Kreme doughnut we taste, every new car's contour we run our hand over…we want it or more of it.

I love the *Veggie Tales* animated videos for kids by Big Idea Productions. One of my favorites is "Madame Blueberry and the Stuffmart." It is so spot-on to what I am saying about the love of money and greed. You probably know some kids who have the DVD. Borrow it and see if you do not agree. A word of warning, once you watch one, you will be hooked and want to see them all.

For me, greed was not really as strong or powerful in my life as the love of money. I think it was much stronger for some of the victims. Wanting more and more was not really what it was about in my life. The reason, I believe, is because one of my spiritual gifts is generosity.

From a very early age, actually as far back as I can remember, I was taught to be generous by my parents. There was an elderly woman—a *spinster*, I think, would be the appropriate older term for her—who lived alone across the street from us when I was growing up. Bessie Carpenter was her name. We called her Miss Bessie. My mom and dad looked after her. My mom would make her meals, and my dad would take care of things around her house for her.

As she aged and her health declined, she was no longer able to live by herself. She had no immediate family and had to be put into a nursing home. My dad continued to look after her dog and parrot, but without her there, they died soon after she left. Every Sunday after church, we went to visit her. Eventually I do not think she even knew we were there, but we went anyway. We went faithfully every week. I remember as a kid hating to go. It was boring sitting still for what seemed like forever, but I am sure it was not more than an hour.

I remember the night Miss Bessie passed in the summer of 1975. We were at a friend's house for a cookout. This was before cell phones, so somehow, someone tracked us down to tell us Miss Bessie would not last much longer. She was no longer in the nursing home but was in the hospital. We left immediately, hurrying in our efforts to get to the hospital in time. We had a flat tire along the way, but my dad never stopped. My brothers and I stayed in the car while my parents went in. We were too late; she had passed away all alone. I was so sad! We loved Miss Bessie as though she were our own grandmother or great aunt.

I look back now and cherish those visits I was forced to endure week after week and the lessons that those visits taught me. That sweet lady along with my parents taught me the importance of being generous with not just your money but with your time as well. My parents were quiet with their generosity, not wanting any recognition. Both embodied great examples of humility as well. Still, when you have the spiritual gift of generosity—or any spiritual gift, for that matter—you cannot keep it a secret. Anyone who knows my parents today, if asked one trait that sets them apart, would most likely say their generosity.

Spiritual gifts are not given by the Holy Spirit to be kept under wraps. In fact, as believers, when God gifts us, He also makes those gifts a natural part of His love flowing out of us. We cannot help but use them. Often, we do not even realize we are using them.

My late friend Ace had the gift of service or helping others. He naturally saw other people's needs, and wherever he was, he would stop to help. We would be out to eat, and he would disappear across the restaurant because he saw a need to help a total stranger. If we were having a meal at church, Ace was the first to start cleaning up. It was natural to him. He could *not* not help. My late uncle Johnny, whom we called Uncle Goat because of his white billy goat beard, had the same gift. He too could not wait to help others.

Generosity is one of my gifts, and I cannot help but be generous. Generosity is different from service or helping others. Generosity, in simple terms, is the willingness to give the very shirt off your back to someone to meet their need, even if it means you have to go without. That is me. I love being able to meet others' needs.

Countless times, I have paid power bills, grocery bills, rent, student loans, bought cars, loaned cars, volunteered time, opened up our house to moms with children, let people stay rent-free in houses I owned, and traveled to Gulfport, Mississippi, for a year doing Hurricane Katrina relief work. I do not like even talking about this stuff because I believe we should not toot our own horn. God knows the things we do for others, and we should not let the right hand know what the left hand is doing. However, it needs to be said here because you need to know my heart, my unseen actions, to understand who I really am, not who you think I am because of the sins in my life, or what the media chooses to say, or what others' opinions of me get put online.

Wait. Let me go ahead and say it now, because I hear so many victims crying, "*Foul!* It is easy to be generous with someone else's money!"

And I say, "No, it is not."

Greedy people do not do these things. Always and forever, everything is about themselves, never about others. That is not me.

Here is another example. A man whom we knew through homeschooling and the Christian Athletic Association (CAA) came to me for help. His daughter was about to marry a young man who was about to inherit control over a trust worth several million dollars. When he was a young boy, he was the sole survivor of an automobile accident that claimed the lives of his parents. He was raised by his grandparents. The car manufacturer was found to be at fault, and he was awarded the trust. At age eighteen, he received control of about $3 million and would, over the next few years, receive several more. His relatives were lining up like wolves to get their share for helping raise him. He did not know what to do. He did not like the trustees who were handling the money, and he wanted to move it. His future father-in-law wanted to help the young man. He came to me. Could I help?

I know what you are thinking. Of course I could help, just write BFG a check for three million, and all would be well. Nope, not what happened. Oh, I could have, and he would have done it. Nope, I called a lady at my bank and asked her to set up a meeting with their trust department. We all met. They made a proposal. The young man accepted, and as far as I know, he still uses their services to this day. I did not receive a penny for helping.

I ask you, does that sound like a greedy, lowlife mastermind—a cheating, thieving criminal—to you?

I said earlier, greed would be more associated with some of the victims. That was not an accusation as much as an observation. Here is an example: I will call him Mr. B, and his son, Mr. K. Mr. B and Mr. K personify what I am talking about. They came to me because they heard about the great returns other people were getting, how happy they were, and they wanted in. They wanted in but were also skeptical and apprehensive. I told them like I told everyone, "You have to be able to sleep at night with your decision. If you are losing sleep over it, then it does not matter how much interest you are making, it is not worth it; so do not do it." They could not stand it. They could not turn down the returns or stand the thoughts of someone else getting the great returns and them being left out, so they invested several hundred thousand dollars. Mrs. B kept worrying Mr. B and Mr. K about it. Every time I saw Mr. B in the Claremont Café, he drilled me on how things were going. He and Mr. K needed lots of TLC, lots of handholding. Finally, I sent them a letter and individual checks closing out their accounts. I explained they obviously were losing sleep over their decision, and I felt it best if they went someplace else to invest. You may not think that sounds like greed on their part, and I would agree. Then, I got a phone call from Mr. B begging me to take him back. I told him no. Every time he saw me at the Claremont Café, he asked if I would please take him back. Again, I said no. But he needed the interest! Nothing else was paying as much. He had to have it! He wanted it! Still, I said no.

I ask you again, does that sound like a greedy, lowlife mastermind—a cheating, thieving criminal—to you? Does that sound like greed on Mr. B's part?

Here is another example. I did not do IRAs. I could not. BFG was not an approved institution, nor could it be an approved institution to take IRA money. However, people were constantly begging me to find a way to get approved. They could not stand the thought of losing out on the interest.

I admit, I felt the temptation of greed, and at times I would have to say I was guilty of the sin. But to say I acted solely out of a greedy character and was a greedy person would be a mistake.

I do not think greedy people care about the people they hurt or who they have to run over to get what they want. I know it sounds terrible and unbelievable, but I did care about the victims. I hated this whole ugly business—and still do. I prayed for my clients and sometimes with them in my office. I cried with the husbands as they shared their struggles with wives who were suffering from cancer. I wept with the parents whose teenage son died of cancer and with the grandmother who lost a grandson to a car accident.

How could I say that, and yet, with a smile on my face, take more and more, and spend more and more?

It makes no sense. I know and I agree. I cannot fully explain it. All I know is that it is true. When I say I felt trapped and could not get out or stop it, it is true. I am not making that up to rationalize my actions or garner your sympathy. Some things, however improbable or incredible, are still true; we just have to accept them. We are all like water; we seek to flow the path of least resistance. For me, it was easier to perpetuate the business than to put everyone through the pain of bringing it to an end, but that in itself is a fallacy as well. There is no happy ending for anyone perpetuating the business. Better to cut the head off the serpent while it is a baby rather than a full-grown monster.

Obviously, hindsight is always twenty-twenty; and if I could go back, I would change things. Alas, I cannot. All I can do going forward is try to make amends any way I can. That is what I want to do.

People ask where I go from here. I do not know 100 percent what the future holds. None of us do. I do have some dreams, and some of them change. When my wife got cancer and died, that single event changed some of my dreams and hopes. I have a lot of faith that God is not through with me—not by a long shot, both in prison and out. I do hope that the *out* comes sooner rather than later. I have never believed God intends for me to spend thirty years in prison, but if He does, I accept that. I am not happy about it, but after all, He is sovereign and I completely trust Him with everything in my life.

I would also be a liar if I said I did not have days when my patience runs very thin. That is when I have to really buckle down in prayer and seek His peace. I have days when I feel the walls closing in on me to the point of feeling like a panic attack is coming on. I wake up almost screaming from nightmares of reliving those seventeen years. God is always faithful and steadfast in His love for me at these times. It is then that He prompts someone to send me a card of encouragement to let me know how much He loves me and that I am not forgotten. I pray for that same comfort for all the victims, because I am certain some of them experience their own anxiety and nightmares as well.

I have some ideas and dreams I would like to see fulfilled someday. I would like to write more books, both fiction and nonfiction. I would like to start several businesses. However, my three greatest passions are becoming a national public speaker, ministering to college students, and starting a national ministry to help break the cycle that keeps perpetuating the succession of inmates in families. I want to intercede in the lives of young children who are doomed to a life of incarceration, as have all the males in their families.

Following the initial publishing of this book, I plan to apply to the Governor's Office of Executive Clemency for a reduction in time. The governor can grant me either clemency or a full pardon. I am not seeking a full pardon. A full pardon wipes the slate clean as if there was never a crime committed. That means all your rights under the Constitution are restored. I do not feel I deserve a full pardon at this time. At some point in the future, when I have proven myself worthy of that honor, then I may apply for it. For now, I do intend to apply for clemency on these last four sentences. I had six consecutive sixty- to eighty-one-month sentences. I finished the first two sentences by November 2018 and am currently serving the third, which will end November 2023. The other three are to follow in order of succession. I will be sixty years old by the time the current sentence ends, will have served fifteen years, and will have cost the taxpayers nearly half a million dollars to feed, clothe, house, provide medical care, and protect me.

I have waited to apply for clemency because it was important to me for the receiver to finish his work, for the civil lawsuits to be over, to not appear indifferent to the feelings of the victims, and to complete this book. I am sure there will still be those, like Barry and Glenda, who will be adamant that even thirty years is not enough; but I am equally sure there will be even more who will agree that enough is enough.

If you wish to contact me, go to the website for the North Carolina Department of Public Safety, follow the links to the inmate locator, and search for my current location and the address for the facility. If you write, please make sure to include my OPUS number (1188382) next to my name.

I invite you to join me in praying Proverbs 21:1: "The king's heart is a stream of water in the hand of the LORD; he turns it wherever he will." I am praying this verse for the North Carolina governor and his Office of Executive Clemency as they review my application.

I leave you with these verses to ponder:

> So we do not lose heart. Though our outer self is wasting away, our inner self is being renewed day by day. For this light momentary affliction is preparing for us an eternal weight of glory beyond all comparison, as we look not to the things that are seen but the things that are unseen. For the things that are seen are transient, but the things that are unseen are eternal. (2 Corinthians 4:16–18)

> Search me, O God, and know my heart! Try me and know my thoughts! And see if there be

any grievous way in me, and lead me in the way everlasting! (Psalm 139:23–24)

Amen and amen!

Bibliography

Thomas, C. (1993, July 27). *LA Times*.

About the Author

J. V. Huffman Jr. was born in Claremont in 1963 and graduated from Bunker Hill High School. After graduating, he attended Lenoir-Rhyne College (now Lenoir-Rhyne University), where in 1985 he received a BA in international business. Postgraduation, he married his high school sweetheart, Gilda Bolick. They raised four children and have eight grandchildren. After thirty-three years of marriage, Gilda went home to be with the Lord in 2018 after a yearlong battle with acute myeloid leukemia.

He served six years on the Catawba County Board of Education as well as on the Catawba County Board of Adjustments. He also served on various advisory and nonprofit boards over the years.

JV is currently serving a prison sentence of over thirty years for running a seventeen-year long Ponzi scheme, which you will learn more about in this book.

www.ingramcontent.com/pod-product-compliance
Lightning Source LLC
Chambersburg PA
CBHW022016150726
47990CB00002B/675